NOTES AND COUNTER-NOTES

Other works by Eugène Ionesco

EUGENE IONESCO

NOTES AND COUNTER-NOTES

Translated from the French by
Donald Watson

LONDON
JOHN CALDER

FIRST PUBLISHED IN 1964 BY
JOHN CALDER (PUBLISHERS) LTD
17 SACKVILLE STREET, LONDON W.I.

ORIGINALLY PUBLISHED IN FRANCE BY
EDITIONS GALLIMARD, 1962, UNDER THE TITLE *Notes et contre-notes*.

PRINTED IN GT. BRITAIN BY
BALDING + MANSELL, WISBECH

CONTENTS

PREFACE

There are many repetitions in this book. This is not entirely my fault; it is also the fault of all those journalists, interviewers, specialists and politicians in the theatre who, always a prey to the same obsessions, have been hurling the same fundamental criticisms at me for years; criticisms which I, in my turn try to answer by arguments that are always the same. Actually, I have been fighting chiefly to safeguard my freedom to think, my freedom as a writer. It is clear that for the most part it has been a dialogue between the deaf, for walls do not have ears and people have become walls to one another: no-one discusses anything with anyone nowadays, as everyone wants to gain a disciple or crush an opponent.

I rather regret that I have tried to give an answer, that I have constructed theories and talked too much, when it was my business simply to 'invent' and pay no attention to the touts who kept tugging at my sleeve. I have almost fallen into the trap they set me and I have often given way to the temptation of polemics. Not that one should avoid polemics. But a work of art should contain within itself and crystallise arguments of much greater complexity, which it examines and answers far more thoroughly.

Although I was hoping to defend myself, my defence may not do me much good. By that I mean I have wasted too much time in the attempt; yet I had to try and explain that other people's explanations were tendentious and therefore misleading. I may also have attached too much importance to my own plays, but there too I have an excuse, for other people have made my work out to be important. In any case these *Notes*

and Counter-Notes reflect a day-by-day struggle; they were
written in the heat of battle. Perhaps they will be able to serve as
documentary evidence, revealing what kind of questions or
criticisms can be aimed at a writer at the present time and also
what sort of views can be held by a harassed author who, in
trying to defend himself on all fronts at once, sometimes gets
caught out in contradictions which will surely be noticed by
his readers and for which he offers his apologies.

And yet a fair number of my critics have become friends,
after living and arguing our way together through this ten or
twelve-year period. We are bound to one another and now,
when I write a play, I cannot help thinking of one or other of
them; they are a reflection of my real public and, whether I
want to or not, I am really still thinking about them when I
write and ask myself what they are going to say and what their
reaction will be when they see 'this one'.

I must confess I soon forget favourable reviews: it is the
unfavourable ones that stand out, those are the ones that linger
in the mind. In any case the pages of *Notes and Counter-Notes*
devoted to the critics are not, in spite of everything, an expression of private pique, or only very slightly. They rather tend to
illustrate Jean Paulhan's thesis that criticism is impossible: no
theoretically, but in my own more simple way, by means of
living examples and precise quotations that attempt to throw
light on the difficult question of judgement, on the lack of critical standards, and on the illogicalities that arise from emotional
involvement in present-day problems, tangled affirmations and
denials that cancel each other out. In the following pages much
is said, as much is said around us, about incommunicability or
the crisis of language. This crisis is most often artificially and
deliberately produced. Propaganda has consciously obscured

the meaning of words in order to throw our minds into confusion. It is a modern method of warfare. When it is maintained
that white is black and black is white, it is indeed very difficult
to find one's way about. Sometimes I note the deliberate defor-
mation or destruction of language and I denounce it; I also note
its natural tendency to wear out; again I note how mechanical
it becomes, so that language gets separated from life; I imagine
therefore that it is not so much necessary to re-invent it as to
restore it. Perhaps this comes to the same thing, but bad faith
is obviously the greatest danger of all. And I realise, for example, that it was very simple-minded of me to insist on trying
to prove that there can be some disinterested activities, when
this is known already by anyone who has ever played football
or cards or chess or snakes and ladders, etc . . . But politicians do
not want theatrical activity to be disinterested and gratuitous;
they hate it to be free and escape from them. It was therefore a
considerable waste of energy on my part to linger so long over
these questions. But in the last resort, as everything is gratuitous
— even non-gratuitousness — let us say I was still acting
gratuitously.

Perhaps my plays do go a little further than my own comments on the plays; I hope that, in spite of myself, they do say
more, for if they really were to be completely exhausted by my
arguments, entirely contained in them, they would not be of
very great value.

But if literature has any importance, if it is to be of importance today and in the future, there is another agonising
problem. The new world that seems to be opening ahead of us,
a perspective either of death or, on the contrary, a total transformation of life and thought, seems bound to lead us into an
era in which the very existence of this kind of activity will be

called in question. We cannot predict what forms poetry, creation and art will take. In any case, already at this very moment, literature is not measuring up to life: artistic expression is too feeble, imagination is too impoverished to simulate the horror and the wonder of this life, or of death, too inadequate even to take stock of it. Meanwhile, meanwhile I have done what I could . . . I have passed the time. But we need to know how to cut ourselves off from ourselves and from other people, how to observe and how to laugh, in spite of everything to laugh.

I hope there is more humour in my drama than in my polemics. I sincerely hope so.

E.I.

1. EXPERIENCE OF THE THEATRE

EXPERIENCE OF THE THEATRE

When I am asked the question: 'Why do you write plays?' I always feel very awkward and have no idea what to answer. Sometimes it seems to me that I started writing for the theatre because I hated it. I used to enjoy reading literature and essays and I used to go to the cinema. Occasionally I would listen to music and visit the art galleries; but I can almost say I never went to the theatre.

When I did go, it was quite by accident, to keep someone company or because I had been unable to turn down an invitation, because I *had* to go.

It gave me no pleasure or feeling of participation. The acting embarrassed me: I was embarrassed for the actors. The situations seemed to me quite arbitrary. I felt there was something phoney about it all.

A theatrical performance had no magic for me. Everything seemed rather ridiculous, rather painful. For example, it was beyond me how anyone could dream of being an actor. It seemed to me that actors were doing something unacceptable and reprehensible. They gave up their own personalities, repudiated themselves, changed their own skins. How *could* they consent to being someone else and take on a character different from their own? For me it was a kind of vulgar trick, transparent, inconceivable.

Besides, an actor did not even become someone else, he just pretended, which was, I thought, far worse. I found this very distressing and in a kind of way dishonest. 'What a good actor', the audience used to say. In my view, he was a bad actor, and acting was a Bad Thing.

For me, going to a public performance meant going to see apparently serious people making a public exhibition of themselves. And yet I am not one of those completely matter-of-fact types. I am not opposed to make-believe. On the contrary, I have always considered imaginative truth to be more profound, more loaded with significance, than everyday reality. Realism, socialist or not, never looks beyond reality. It narrows it down, diminishes it, falsifies it, and leaves out of account the obsessive truths that are most fundamental to us: love, death and wonder. It presents man in a perspective that is narrow and alien; truth lies in our dreams, in our imagination: every moment of our lives confirms this statement. Fiction preludes science. Everything we dream about, and by that I mean everything we desire, is true (the myth of Icarus came before aviation, and if Ader or Blériot started flying, it is because all men have dreamt of flight). There is nothing truer than myth: history, in its attempt to 'realise' myth, distorts it, stops half way; when history claims to have 'succeeded', this is nothing but humbug and mystification. Everything we dream is 'realisable'. Reality does not have to be: it is simply what it is. It is the dreamer, the thinker or the scientist who is the revolutionary; it is he who tries to change the world.

The fictional element in the novel did not worry me at all and I accepted it in the cinema. I can believe as naturally in the potential reality of fiction as in my own dreams. Film acting did not fill me with the same indefinable malaise, the same embarrassment as acting in the theatre.

Why could I not accept the truth of theatrical reality? Why did it seem false to me? And why did the false seem to want to pass as true and take the place of truth? Was it the fault of the actors? Of the text? Or my own fault? I think I realise now that what worried me in the theatre was the presence of characters in flesh and blood on the stage. Their physical presence destroyed the imaginative illusion. It was as though there were two planes of reality, the concrete, physical, impoverished, empty and limited reality of these ordinary human beings living, moving and speaking on the stage, and the reality of imagination, face to face, overlapping, irreconcilable: two antagonistic worlds failing to come together and unite.

Yes, that was it: every gesture, every attitude, every speech spoken on the stage destroyed for me a world that these same gestures, attitudes and speeches were specifically designed to evoke; destroyed it even before it could be created. It seemed to me an absolute abortion, a fatal mistake, sheer fatuity. If you stop up your ears to shut out the dance music an orchestra is playing but go on watching the dancers, you can see how ridiculous they look, how fantastic their movements are; in the same way, if someone was present for the first time at the celebration of some religious rite, the whole ceremony would seem to him incomprehensible and absurd.

It was in a spirit you might call unsanctified that I paid my rare visits to the theatre, and that was why I did not like it, did not respond to it, did not believe in it.

In a novel you are *told* a story; it does not matter whether it is invented or not, nothing stops you believing it. In a film you are *shown* a fictional story; it is a novel in pictures, an illustrated novel. So a film too tells a story; of course, the fact that it is visual in no way changes this and you can still believe it. Music is a combination of notes, a story in notes, adventures in sound. A painting is an organisation or a disorganisation of forms, colours and planes, and the question of belief or disbelief does not arise; it is there, as evidence: all that is required is that these various elements satisfy the exacting ideals of composition and pictorial expression. The novel, music and painting are pure structural form, containing no elements that are extraneous; that is why they can stand alone, they are admissible. Even the cinema can be accepted, because it is a succession of pictures, which means that it too is pure, whereas the theatre seemed to me essentially impure: the fictional element was mixed with others that were foreign to it; it was imperfectly fictional, yes, raw material that had not yet undergone the transformation or mutation that is indispensable. In short, everything about the theatre exasperated me. When I saw actors, for example, identifying themselves completely with their parts and weeping real tears on the stage, I found it unbearable, positively indecent.

When on the other hand I saw an actor who was too much in control of his part, out of character, dominating it, detached from it, which was what Diderot and Jouvet and Piscator and, after him, Brecht all wanted, I was just as dissatisfied. This too seemed to me an unacceptable mixture of true and false, for I felt a need for the essential transformation or transposition of a reality that only imagination and artistic creation can make more meaningful, more dense, more 'true', that the didactic doctrines of realism merely overload, impoverish and reduce to the level of a second-rate ideology. I did not like stage actors, stars, who for me represented an anarchical principle, breaking up and destroying to their own advantage the organised unity of the stage, attracting all attention to themselves to the detriment of any coherent integration of the elements of drama. But the dehumanisation of the actor, as practised by Piscator or Brecht, a disciple of Piscator, who turned the actor into a simple pawn in the chess game of drama, a lifeless tool, denied passion, participation or personal invention, this time to the advantage of the production, which now, in its turn, attracted all attention to itself, — this priority given to organised unity exasperated me just as much and made me feel, quite literally, that something was being smothered: to squash the actor's initiative, to kill the actor, is to kill both life and drama.

Later, that is to say quite recently, I realised that Jean Vilar had managed to strike the necessary balance in his productions — respecting the need for cohesion on the stage without dehumanising the actor and thus restoring to drama its unity and to the actor his freedom — half way between the style of the *Odéon* (and so an advance on the rantings of a Sarah Bernhardt or a Mounet-Sully) and that of the Brechtian or Piscatoresque discipline. This is not, however, with Vilar an expression of theories about the theatre or hard and fast dogmatism, but a question of tact and instinctive sense of theatre.

But I still could not quite see how to get rid of that positive feeling of malaise produced by my awareness of the 'impurity' of acted drama. I was by no means an agreeable theatregoer, but on the contrary sulky, grumbling, always discontented. Was this due to some deficiency in myself alone? Or was it something lacking in the theatre?

I was dissatisfied even by the plays I had managed to read. Not all of them! For I was not blind to the merits of Sophocles Aeschylus, or Shakespeare, nor a little later to some of the plays of Kleist or Büchner. Why? Because, I thought, all these plays make extraordinary reading on account of their literary qualities, which may well not be specifically theatrical. In any case, after Shakespeare and Kleist, I do not think I have enjoyed reading a play. Strindberg seemed to me clumsy and inadequate. Even Molière bored me. I was not interested in those stories of misers, hypocrites and cuckolds. I disliked his unmetaphysical mind. Shakespeare raised questions about the whole condition and destiny of man. In the long run Molière's little problems seemed to me of relatively minor importance, sometimes a little sad of course, dramatic even, but never tragic; for they could be resolved. The unendurable admits of no solution, and only the unendurable is profoundly tragic, profoundly comic and essentially theatrical.

On the other hand, the greatness of Shakespeare's plays seemed to me diminished in performance. No Shakespearian production ever captivated me as much as my reading of *Hamlet*, *Othello* and *Julius Caesar* etc. As I went so rarely to the theatre, perhaps I have never seen the best productions of Shakespeare's drama? In any case, in performance I had the impression that the unendurable had been made endurable. It was anguish tamed.

So I am really not a passionate theatregoer, still less a man of the theatre. I really hated the theatre. It bored me. And yet . . . when I was a child, I can still remember how my mother could not drag me away from the Punch and Judy show in the Luxembourg Gardens. I would go there day after day and could stay there, spellbound, all day long. But I did not laugh. That Punch and Judy show kept me there open-mouthed, watching those puppets talking, moving and cudgelling each other. It was the very image of the world that appeared to me, strange and improbable but true as true, in the profoundly simplified form of caricature, as though to stress the grotesque and brutal nature of the truth. And from then until I was fifteen any form of play would thrill me and make me feel that the world is very strange, a feeling so deeply rooted that it has never left me. Every live show awoke in me this feeling for the strangeness of the world, and it impressed me nowhere more than at the theatre. And yet, when I was thirteen, I wrote a play, my first piece of writing, which had nothing strange about it. It was a patriotic play: extreme youth is an excuse for anything.

When did I stop liking the theatre? From the moment when, as I began to grow more clear-sighted and acquire a critical mind, I became conscious of stage tricks, of obvious theatrical contrivance, that is to say from the moment I stopped being naïve. Where are the *monstres sacrés* of the theatre who could give us back our lost naïvety? And what possible magic could justify the theatre's claim to bind us in its spell? There is no magic now, nothing is sacred: there is no valid reason for this to be restored to us.

Besides, there is nothing more difficult than writing for the theatre. Novels and poems last well. Their appeal is not blunted even by the centuries. We still find interest in a number of minor works from the nineteenth, eighteenth and seventeenth centuries. And how many even older works do we not still find interesting? All painting and music resists the passage of time. The moving simplicity of the least significant sculptured heads on countless cathedrals still remains fresh and alive, intact; and we shall go on responding to the architectural rhythms of great monuments to the most distant civilisations, which speak to us directly through them in a language that is clear and revealing. But what of the theatre?

To-day the theatre is blamed by some for not belonging to its own times. In my view it belongs only too well. This is what makes it so weak and ephemeral. I mean that the theatre *does* belong to its own times, but not quite enough. Every period needs something 'out of period' and incommunicable to be introduced into what is 'period' and communicable.

Everything is a circumscribed moment in history, of course. But all history is contained in each moment of history: any moment in history is valid when it transcends history; in the particular lies the universal.

The themes chosen by many authors merely spring from a certain ideological fashion, which is something *less* than the period it belongs to. Or else these themes are the expression of some particular political attitude, and the plays that illustrate them will die with the ideology that has inspired them, for ideologies go out of fashion. Any Christian tomb, any Greek or Etruscan stele moves us and tells us more about the destiny of man than any number of laboriously committed plays, which are made to serve a discipline, a system of thought and language different from what is properly their own.

It is true that all authors have tried to make propaganda. The great ones are those who failed, who have gained access, consciously or not, to a deeper and more universal reality. Nothing is more precarious than a play. It may maintain its position for a very short time, but it soon falls apart, revealing nothing but contrivance.

In all sincerity Corneille bores me. Perhaps we like him (without believing in him) only from habit. We cannot help it. He has been forced on us at school. I find Schiller unbearable. For a long time now, Marivaux's plays have seemed to me futile little comedies. Musset's are thin and Vigny's unactable. Victor Hugo's bloody dramas send us into fits of laughter; whereas it is difficult to laugh, whatever people say, at most of Labiche's funny plays. Dumas fils, with his *Dame aux Camélias*, is ridiculously sentimental. As for the others! Oscar Wilde? Facile. Ibsen? Boorish. Strindberg? Clumsy. A recent dramatist, Giraudoux, not long dead, does not always get across the footlights now; like Cocteau's, his drama seems to us superficial and contrived. It has lost its sparkle: with Cocteau the theatrical tricks are too obvious; with Giraudoux the tricks and contrivances of language, distinguished though they be, still remain tricks.

Pirandello himself has been left behind the times, for his theatre was built on theories about personality or the multiformity of truth, which now seem clear as daylight since psycho-analysis and psychology plumbed the depths. In testing the validity of Pirandello's theories, modern psychology, inevitably going further than Pirandello in its exploration of the human psyche, certainly confirms Pirandello's findings, but at the same time shows him to be limited and inadequate: for what has been said by Pirandello is now said more thoroughly and scientifically. So the value of his theatre does not rest on his contribution to psychology but on the quality of his drama, which must inevitably lie elsewhere: what interests us in this author is no longer the discovery of the antagonistic elements in human personality, but what he has made of them dramatically. The strictly theatrical interest of his work lies outside science, beyond the limits of his own ideology. All that is left of Pirandello is his dramatic technique, the mechanics of his theatre: which again proves that drama founded on ideology or philosophy, exclusively inspired by them, is built on sand and crumbles away. It is his dramatic idiom, his purely theatrical instinct that keeps Pirandello alive for us to-day.

In the same way, it is not Racine's psychological insight into the passions that sustains his theatre; but what Racine has made of it as a poet and man of the theatre.

If we were to go through the centuries and count the dramatists who can still move an audience, we should find about twenty . . . or at the most thirty. But the paintings, poems and novels that still mean something to us can be counted in their thousands. The naïvety essential to a work of art is lacking in the theatre. I do not say a dramatist of great simplicity will not appear; but at the moment I see no sign of him on the horizon. I mean a simplicity that is lucid, springing from the inmost depths of our being, revealing them, revealing them to ourselves, restoring our own simplicity, our secret souls. At the moment there is no naïvety, in audience or writer.

What faults are there then to be found in dramatists and their plays? Their tricks, I was saying, that is to say their too obvious contrivances. The theatre may appear to be a secondary, a minor form of literature. It always seems rather coarse-grained. There is no doubt it is an art that deals in effects. It cannot do without them, and this is the reproach levelled against it. And these effects have to be broad. One has the impression that the texture has been roughened. The textual refinement of literature is obscured. Drama of literary subtlety soon wears thin. Half tones are deepened or banished by light that is too brilliant. No shading, no nuance is possible. Problem plays, *pièces à thèse*, are rough approximations. Drama is not the idiom for ideas. When it tries to become a vehicle for ideologies, all it can do is vulgarise them. It dangerously over-simplifies. It makes them too elementary and depreciates them. It is 'naïve', but in the bad sense. All ideological drama runs the risk of being parochial. What would, not the *utility*, but the proper *function* of the theatre be, if it was restricted to the task of duplicating philosophy or theology or politics or pedagogy? Psychological drama is not psychological enough. One might as well read a psychological treatise. Ideological drama is not philosophical enough. Instead of going to see a dramatic illustration of this or that political creed I would rather read my usual daily paper or listen to the speeches of my party candidates.

Dissatisfied with the gross naïvety and rudimentary character of the theatre, philosophers, literary men, ideologists and poets of refinement, all intelligent people try to make their drama intelligent. They write with intelligence, with taste and talent. They put their thoughts into it, they express their conception of life and the world, and believe that writing a play should be like presenting a thesis in which problems find their solution on the stage. They sometimes construct their work in the form of a syllogism, with the two premises in the first two acts and the conclusion in the third.

There is no denying the construction is sometimes first-rate. And yet this does not answer the demands we make of drama, because it fails to lift the theatre out of an intermediate zone that lies somewhere between art where discursive reasoning can be only one ingredient — and the higher realms of thought.

Should one give up the theatre, if one refuses to reduce it to a parochial level or subordinate it to manifestations of the human spirit that impose different forms and modes of expression? Can it, like painting or music, find its own autonomous existence?

Drama is one of the oldest of the arts. And I can't help thinking we cannot do without it. We cannot resist the desire to people a stage with live characters that are at the same time real and invented. We cannot deny our need to make them speak and live before our eyes. To bring phantoms to life and give them flesh and blood is a prodigious adventure, so unique that I myself was absolutely amazed, during the rehearsals of my first play, when I suddenly saw, moving on the stage of the

'*Noctambules*', characters who owed their life to me. It was a terrifying experience. What right had I to do a thing like that? Was it allowed? And how could Nicolas Bataille, one of my actors, turn into Mr Martin? . . . It was almost diabolical. And so it was only when I had written something for the theatre, quite by chance and with the intention of holding it up to ridicule, that I began to love it, to rediscover it in myself, to understand it, to be fascinated by it: and then I knew what I had to do.

I told myself that the too intelligent playwrights were not intelligent enough: that it was no good thinkers looking to the theatre for the idiom of a philosophical treatise; that when they tried to bring too much subtlety and refinement into the theatre it was not only too much but not enough; that if the theatre was merely a deplorable enlargement of refined subtleties, which I found so embarrassing, it merely meant that the enlargement was not sufficient. The over-large was not large enough, the unsubtle was too subtle.

So if the essence of the theatre lay in magnifying its effects, they had to be magnified still further, underlined and stressed to the maximum. To push drama out of that intermediate zone where it is neither theatre nor literature is to restore it to its own domain, to its natural frontiers. It was not for me to conceal the devices of the theatre, but rather make them still more evident, deliberately obvious, go all out for caricature and the grotesque, way beyond the pale irony of witty drawing-room comedies. No drawing-room comedies, but farce, the extreme exaggeration of parody. Humour, yes, but using the methods of burlesque. Comic effects that are firm, broad and outrageous. No dramatic comedies either. But back to the unendurable. Everything to raised paroxysm, where the source of tragedy lies.

A theatre of violence: violently comic, violently dramatic.

Avoid psychology or rather give it a metaphysical dimension. Drama lies in extreme exaggeration of the feelings, an exaggeration that dislocates flat everyday reality. Dislocation, disarticulation of language too.

Moreover, if the actors embarrassed me by not seeming natural enough, perhaps it was because they too were or tried to be *too* natural: by trying not to be, perhaps they will still appear natural, but in a different way. They must not be afraid of not being natural.

We need to be virtually bludgeoned into detachment from our daily lives, our habits and mental laziness, which conceal from us the strangeness of the world. Without a fresh virginity of mind, without a new and healthy awareness of existential reality, there can be no theatre and no art either; the real must be in a way dislocated, before it can be reintegrated.

To achieve this effect, a trick can sometimes be used: playing against the text. A serious, solemn, formal production or interpretation can be grafted onto a text that is absurd, wild and comic. On the other hand, to avoid the ridiculous sentimentality of the tear-jerker, a dramatic text can be treated as buffoonery and the tragic feeling of a play can be underlined by farce. Light makes shadows darker, shadows intensify light. For my part, I have never understood the difference people make between the comic and the tragic. As the 'comic' is an intuitive perception of the absurd, it seems to me more hopeless than the 'tragic'. The 'comic' offers no escape. I say 'hopeless', but in reality it lies outside the boundaries of hope or despair.

Tragedy may appear to some in one sense comforting, for in trying to express the helplessness of a beaten man, one broken by fate for example, tragedy thus admits the reality of fate and destiny, of sometimes incomprehensible but objective laws that govern the universe. And man's helplessness, the futility of our efforts, can also, in a sense, appear comic.

I have called my comedies 'anti-plays' or 'comic dramas', and my dramas 'pseudo-dramas' or 'tragic farces': for it seems to me that comic and tragic are one, and that the tragedy of man is pure derision. The contemporary critical mind takes nothing too seriously or too lightly. In *Victimes du Devoir* I tried to sink comedy in tragedy: in *Les Chaises* tragedy in comedy or, if you like, to confront comedy and tragedy in order to link them in a new dramatic synthesis. But it is not a true synthesis, for these two elements do not coalesce, they coexist: one constantly repels the other, they show each other up, criticise and deny one another and, thanks to their opposition, thus succeed dynamically in maintaining a balance and creating tension. The two plays that best satisfy this condition are, I believe: *Victimes du Devoir* and *Le Nouveau Locataire*.

Similarly one can confront the prosaic and the poetic, the strange and the ordinary. That is what I wanted to do in *Jacques ou la Soumission*, which I called 'a *naturalistic* comedy' too, because after starting off in a naturalistic tone I tried to go beyond naturalism.

In the same way *Amédée ou comment s'en débarrasser*, where the scene is laid in the flat of a *petit bourgeois* couple, is a realistic play into which fantastic elements have been introduced, a contrast intended at one and the same time to banish and recall the 'realism'.

In my first play, *La Cantatrice chauve*, which started off as an attempt to parody the theatre, and hence a certain kind of human behaviour, it was by plunging into banality, by draining the sense from the hollowest clichés of everyday language that I tried to render the strangeness that seems to pervade our whole existence. The tragic and the farcical, the prosaic and the poetic, the realistic and the fantastic, the strange and the ordinary, perhaps these are the contradictory principles (there is no theatre without conflict) that may serve as a basis for a new dramatic structure. In this way perhaps the unnatural can by its very violence appear natural, and the too natural will avoid the naturalistic.

May I add that 'primitive' drama is not elementary drama; to refuse to 'round off the corners' is a way of providing a clear outline, a more powerful shape; drama that relies on simple effects is not necessarily drama simplified.

If one believes that 'theatre' merely means the drama of the word, it is difficult to grant it can have an autonomous language of its own: it can then only be the servant of other forms of thought expressed in words, of philosophy and morals. Whereas, if one looks on the word as only *one* member of the shock-troops the theatre can marshal, everything is changed. First of all, there is a proper way for the theatre to use words, which is as dialogue, words in action, words in conflict. If they are used by some authors merely for discussion, this is a major error. There are other means of making words more theatrical: by working them up to such a pitch that they reveal the true temper of drama, which lies in frenzy; the whole tone should be as strained as possible, the language should almost break up or explode in its fruitless effort to contain so many meanings.

But the theatre is more than words: drama is a story that is lived and relived with each performance, and we can watch it live. The theatre appeals as much to the eye as to the ear. It is not a series of pictures, like the cinema, but architecture, a moving structure of scenic images.

Nothing is barred in the theatre: characters may be brought
to life, but the unseen presence of our inner fears can also be
materialised. So the author is not only allowed, but recom-
mended to make actors of his props, to bring objects to life, to
animate the scenery and give symbols concrete form.

Just as the words are complemented by gesture, acting and
pantomime, which can take their place when words are no
longer adequate, so they can be amplified by the scenic elements of the stage as well. The use of props is yet another
question. (Artaud had something to say about that.)

When people say that the theatre should be purely social, do
they not really mean that the theatre should be political,
slanted, of course, in this or that direction. It is one thing to be
social; to be 'socialist' or 'marxist' or 'fascist' is another, — this
is the expression of a kind of stock-taking that does not go far
enough: the more I see of Brecht's plays, the more I have the
impression that time, *and* his own time, escape him; Brechtian
man is shorn of one dimension, the writer's sense of period is
actually falsified by his ideology, which narrows his field of
vision; this is a fault common to ideologists and people
stunted by fanaticism.

Then one may be a social being in spite of oneself, since we
are all of us caught in a kind of historical complex and belong
to one special moment in history — which is, however, far from
absorbing us entirely but rather expresses and contains only the
least essential part of us.

I have spoken mainly about a certain technique, about a
theatrical idiom, an idiom which is all its own. Social themes or
subjects may very well form the subject and themes of drama,
if they remain within this idiom. It is perhaps only through

subjectivity that we become objective. The individual is linked to the generality of men, and society is obviously an objective fact: and yet I see this social element, and by that I mean rather the expression of history, of the period we belong to, even if it only appears in our natural idiom (and all idiom too is historical, limited to its own time, that is undeniable), I see this expression of history as being naturally inherent in a work of art, whatever one's conscious intentions, but vital and spontaneous rather than deliberate or ideological.

Besides contemporaneity does not conflict with timelessness and universality: on the contrary, it is subservient.

There are some states of mind, some intuitions that lie positively outside time, outside history. When, one day of grace, I awake some morning, not only from my night's sleep but also from the mental sleep of habit, and suddenly become aware of my existence and of a universal presence, when all seems strange and yet familiar, when I am possessed by the wonder of living, this is a feeling or intuition that can come to any man at any time. You can find this spirit of awareness expressed in practically the same terms by poets, mystics and philosophers, who experience it exactly as I do, and as all men have surely experienced it unless they are spiritually dead or blinded by their preoccupation with politics; you can find exactly the same spirit clearly expressed both in Antiquity and the Middle Ages as well as in any of the so-called 'historical' centuries. At this timeless moment in time philosopher and shoemaker, 'master' and 'slave', priest and layman are reconciled and indistinguishable.

The historical and the non-historical are joined and welded together in poetry and painting too. The identical picture of a woman dressing her hair is found in certain Persian miniatures, in Greek and Etruscan steles and in Egyptian wall-painting; a Renoir or a Manet or painters from the seventeenth and eighteenth centuries did not need to know the paintings of other periods to find and catch the same attitude, imbued with the same unfailing sensual grace and inspiring the same emotion. As with my first example, we are here dealing with permanent emotions. The pictorial style in which the image is rendered differs (though often very little) according to period. But this 'difference', which is of secondary importance, upholds and illumines a permanent value. All the evidence is there to show us how contemporaneity or 'historicity', to use a vogue word, meets and merges with timelessness, universality and super-historicity, how each lends support to the other.

Let us choose a great example in our own field: in the theatre, when the fallen Richard II is a prisoner in his cell, abandoned and alone, it is not Richard II I see there, but all the fallen kings of this world; and not only all fallen kings, but also our beliefs and values, our unsanctified, corrupt and worn-out truths, the crumbling of civilisations, the march of destiny. When Richard II dies, it is really the death of all I hold most dear that I am watching; it is *I* who die with Richard II. Richard II makes me sharply conscious of the eternal truth that we forget in all these stories, the truth we fail to think about, though it is simple and absolutely commonplace: I die, he dies, you die. So it is not history after all that Shakespeare is writing, although he makes use of history; it is not History that he shows me, but *my* story and *our* story — *my* truth, which, independent of my 'times' and in the spectrum of a time that transcends Time, repeats a universal and inexorable truth. In fact, it is in the nature of a dramatic masterpiece to provide a superior pattern of instruction: it reflects my own image, it is a mirror;

it is soul-searching; it is history gazing beyond history towards
the deepest truth. One may find the reasons given by this or
that author for wars and civil strife and struggles for power
true or false, one may or may not agree with these interpretations. But one cannot deny that all those kings have faded
from the scene, that they are dead; and an awareness of this
reality, of this lasting evidence of the ephemeral nature of man,
contrasted with his longing for eternal life, is obviously accom-
panied by the most profound emotion, by the most acute
consciousness of tragedy, passionately felt. Art is the realm of
passion, not of pedagogy; in this tragedy of tragedies we are
concerned with the revelation of the most painful reality; I
learn or reconsider something that has passed from my mind, I
learn it in the only way possible with poetry, by an emotional
participation that is not distorted by mystification and has burst
through the paper dams of ideology and of a narrowly critical
or 'scientific' spirit. I only risk being taken in when I see a play,
not with evidence to *offer*, but with a thesis to *prove*, an
ideological, committed play, a play that is bogus and not true
profoundly and poetically, as only poetry and tragedy can be
true. All men die a lonely death, all values fall into contempt:
that is what Shakespeare tells me. 'Richard's cell is indeed the
cell of all our solitudes.' Perhaps Shakespeare *wanted* to tell the
story of Richard II: if that was all he had told us, *the story of
someone else*, he would not move me. But Richard II's prison is
a truth that has not been swept away with history: its invisible
walls still stand, whereas countless philosophies and ideologies
have vanished for ever. And this truth still holds, because it is
couched in the idiom of living evidence and not of demonstrative and rational judgement; Richard's prison is there in
front of me, more vivid than any demonstration. Drama *is* this

B

eternal and living presence: there is no doubt that it can reproduce the essential structure of tragic truth and theatrical reality. The evidence it offers has nothing to do with the uncertain truth of abstract thought or with the so-called ideological theatre: we are now concerned with the essence of the theatre, with theatrical archetypes, with theatrical idiom. An idiom that has been lost in our own times, when allegory and academic illustration seem to have been substituted for the living image of truth, which must be rediscovered. Every idiom develops, but development and renewal do not mean self-surrender and a change in kind; they mean a constant rediscovery of self, at each historical moment of time. One develops within the framework of one's own personality. The idiom of the theatre can never be anything but the idiom of the theatre.

As the idioms of painting and music have developed, they have always adjusted to the cultural style of their day, but without ever losing their pictorial or musical nature. And the development of painting, for example, has never been anything but a rediscovery of painting, its idiom and its essence. The direction taken by modern painting shows us this clearly. Since Klee, Kandinsky, Mondrian, Braque and Picasso, painting has done nothing but try to shake off all that is not painting: literature, story-telling, history and photography. Painters are trying to rediscover the basic fundamentals of painting, pure form, colour for its own sake. Nor is it in this case a question of aestheticism or what is nowadays rather improperly called formalism, but of the expression of reality in pictorial terms, *in an idiom as revealing as the language of words and sounds.* Even if this first appeared to us as a disintegration of the pictorial idiom, fundamentally it was the ascetic pursuit of purity, the rejection of a parasitic idiom. Similarly, it is only when we have pulled apart the conventional characters in our plays, only when we have broken down a false theatrical idiom, that we can follow the example of painting and try to put it together again — its essential purity restored.

Theatre can be nothing but theatre, although some contemporary specialists in 'theatricology' consider it not true that a thing can be identified with itself — which seems to me the most bewildering and unlikely form of paradox.

For these 'specialists' the theatre, being something different from the theatre, is ideology, allegory, politics, lectures, essays or literature. This is as much an aberration as it would be to claim that music was archaeology, that painting was physics or mathematics; and tennis anything you like but tennis.

Even if you admit that my views are not untrue, you may well tell me they are by no means new. If you went on to say these truths were elementary, I should be delighted, for there is nothing more difficult than the rediscovery of elementary truths, fundamental premisses, or certitudes. Even philosophers go chiefly in search of sound premisses. Elementary truth is precisely what one loses sight of, what one forgets. And that is why we breed confusion, why we fail in mutual understanding.

Besides, what I have just said is not a preconceived theory of dramatic art. It has not come *before*, but *after* my own personal experience of the theatre. Thinking about my own plays, good or bad, has provoked these few ideas. The reflections came afterwards. I have no ideas *before* I write a play. I have them when I have *finished* it, or while I am *not* writing any at all. I believe that artistic creation is spontaneous. It is for me. Once again, all this is chiefly valid for me; but if I could believe I had discovered instinctively in myself the basic framework and permanent character of the objective reality of drama, or thrown even a little light on what the essence of the theatre is, I should be very proud. All ideologies are derived from knowledge that is second-hand, indirect, devious and false; nothing borrowed from others is true for the artist. For an author nicknamed 'avant-garde', I shall earn the reproach of having invented nothing. I believe that as one invents, one discovers, and that invention *is* discovery or *re*-discovery; and it is not my fault if I am taken for an avant-garde author. It is the critics who say so. It is of no importance. This definition is as good as the next. It means nothing at all. It is just a label.

Surrealism is not new either. All it did was discover and bring to light, in the process of reinventing, a certain way of knowing, or certain tendencies in human nature that centuries of rationalism frowned upon and suppressed. What, in short, does surrealism try to release? Love and dreams. How can we have forgotten that man is quickened by love? How not have noticed that we dream? Like all revolutions, the surrealist revolution was a reversion, a restitution, an expression of vital and indispensable spiritual needs. If finally it became too rigid, if one can now talk of academic surrealism, it is because every idiom wears out in the end; a lively tradition hardens into traditionalism, it becomes set in its forms and is 'imitated'; in its turn, it too must be rediscovered: besides, as is well known, surrealism is itself a rejuvenation of romanticism; its origin, or one of its sources, is in the German Romantics' power to dream. An extension of the frontiers of known reality depends upon a rediscovery of method and a rejuvenation of idiom. A genuine avant-garde movement can only be of value if it is more than a fashion. It can only spring from intuitive discovery, followed by a reassessment of neglected models from the past, which require constant rediscovery and rejuvenation. I believe that in recent times we have forgotten what theatre is. And I am not excepting myself; I believe that, step by step, I have discovered it once more for myself, and what I have just described is simply my own experience of the theatre.

Obviously, a large number of problems have not been touched on. It remains to be seen, for example, how it comes about that a playwright like Feydeau, although the technique and mechanics of his theatre are beyond reproach, is not nearly so great as other playwrights whose technique may or may not be so perfect. In one sense, it is because everyone is a philosopher: by that I mean that everyone discovers some part of reality, the part that he can discover for himself. When I say 'philosopher', I do not mean the specialist in philosophy, who merely exploits other peoples' vision of the world. In so far as an artist has a personal apprehension of reality, he is a true philosopher. And his greatness is a result of the breadth, the depth and acuity of his authentically philosophical insight, of his living philosophy. The quality of a work of art directly depends on how 'alive' philosophy is, on the fact that it springs from life and not from abstract thought. A philosophical system withers away as soon as a new philosophy or a new system goes a step further. Works of art, however, which are live philosophies, do not invalidate one another. That is why they can co-exist. The great works of art and the great poets seem to find confirmation, completion and corroboration in one another; Aeschylus is not cancelled out by Calderon, or Shakespeare by Chekov, or Kleist by a Japanese Noh-Noh play. One scientific theory can cancel out another, but the truths found in works of art complement one another. Art seems the best justification for belief in the possibility of a metaphysical liberalism. (*N.R.F.*, February 1958.)

2. OPINION AND CONTROVERSY

A Writer is not a teacher but an inventor.

Only unpopular theatre has any chance of becoming 'popular'.
A 'people's theatre' is not for the people.

A TALK ABOUT THE AVANT-GARDE[1]

I am, it seems, an avant-garde dramatist. It would even seem obvious since I am present here at discussions on the avant-garde theatre. It is all entirely official.

But what does the term avant-garde mean? I am not a Doctor of Theatrology, nor Philosophy, nor Art: nor am I what is commonly called a 'man-of-the-theatre'.

If I have formed certain ideas about the theatre, they refer above all to my theatre for they have sprung from my own creative experience: they are hardly normative, but rather descriptive. I hope, of course, that rules which apply to me will also apply to others, for the others are all contained in each one of us.

In any case, any laws of theatre which I may discover are provisional and mobile; they come after, not before, artistic creation. If I write a new play, my point of view may be profoundly modified. I may be obliged to contradict myself and I may no longer know whether I still think what I think.

I hope, nevertheless, that some fundamental principles may remain upon which I can lean consciously and instinctively. And here again I can only share with you a purely personal experience.

However, so that I would not make any serious blunders, I looked up the word 'avant-garde' in my Larousse dictionary before I came. I found that the avant-garde, or the van-guard, 'are the troops which precede an armed land, sea or air force and prepare the way for its entry into action.'

[1] A talk that inaugurated the *Helsinki Debates on the Avant-Garde Theatre*, organised by the International Theatre Institute, in June 1959.

Thus, by analogy, in the theatre, the avant-garde would consist of a small shock force of dramatists and sometimes directors, followed at a certain distance by the main body of actors, playwrights and producers. This analogy is perhaps valid when we see what Albérès has stated in his book, *L'Aventure intellectuelle du XXe Siècle:* 'by a phenomenon which no one has troubled to explain (and which indeed would seem difficult) literary sensibility (and artistic of course) has always, in our century, preceded the historic events which were later to corroborate them'. Indeed Baudelaire, Kafka, Pirandello ('who took apart the machinery of lofty family sentiments, etc. . .') and Dostoievski were regarded with good reason as writer-prophets.

Thus the avant-garde would seem to be an artistic and cultural phenomenon of a precursory nature, which tallies with its literal meaning. It would be a kind of 'pre-style' indicating and pointing the direction of a change which will triumph in the end, a change which will truly change everything. This amounts to saying that the avant-garde cannot generally be recognised until after the event; when they have succeeded, when the avant-garde writers and artists have acquired a following, when they have founded a prevailing school, a cultural style which is recognised and will conquer an age. Consequently one can only see that there has been an avant-garde when it no longer exists as such, when it has in fact become a rear guard; when it has been joined and even outstripped by the main army. But an army marching towards what?

I prefer to define the avant-garde in terms of opposition and rupture. While most writers, artists and thinkers believe they belong to their time, the revolutionary playwright feels he is running counter to his time. As a matter of fact, thinkers, artists and so on, after a certain time only make use of ossified forms; they feel they are becoming more and more firmly established in some ideological, artistic or social order which to them seems up to date but which in fact is already tottering and yawning with unsuspected cracks. By the very force of circumstances any system, the moment it is established, is already outworn. As soon as a form of expression becomes recognised, it is already out of date. A thing once spoken is already dead, reality lies somewhere beyond it and the thought has become petrified, so to speak. A manner of speaking — and therefore a manner of being — once imposed, or simply accepted, is already unacceptable. An avant-garde man is like an enemy inside a city he is bent on destroying, against which he rebels; for like any system of government, an established form of expression is also a form of oppression. The avant-garde man is the opponent of an existing system. He is a critic of, and not an apologist for, what exists now. It is easy to criticise the past particularly when the prevailing regime is tolerant and encourages you to do it; but this is only to sanctify ossification and kowtow to tyranny or convention.

I am well aware that I have not thrown any light on the problem. The word 'avant-garde' in fact is used with various meanings. It can quite simply be identified with the 'art theatre', that is the theatre which is more literary, exacting and daring than the kind known in France as the 'théâtre du Boulevard'. This, it seems, is what Georges Pillement meant when, in his theatre anthology published in 1946, he divided dramatists into two categories: the writers of the 'comédie du Boulevard' among whom Robert de Flers ranked with François de Curel; and those of the avant-garde which included Claude-André

Puget as well as Passeur, Jean Anouilh and Giraudoux. This seems rather strange today, for the works of these writers are now practically classics. But Maurice Donnay, in his time, as well as Bataille were avant-garde writers since they expressed a rupture, a new departure and an opposing force. They finally merged into the theatrical tradition and that is what must happen to every good avant-gardist. In any case they represented a protest and the proof of this was that at the outset these authors were given a bad reception by the critics, who protested at their protestations. The protestations of an avant-garde dramatist can be a reaction against Realism when that is the most prevalent and abused form of expression in the theatre; it can be a protest against a certain Symbolism when that Symbolism has become abused, arbitrary and no longer captures reality. In any case what we call the avant-garde theatre, which coexists with the conventional theatre, seems by its expression, its questing nature and difficulty to be more exacting. For the very reason that it is exacting and difficult to follow, it is obvious that before it becomes generally accepted it can only be the theatre of a minority. The avant-garde theatre, and indeed all new art and theatre must be unpopular.

It is certain that any attempt to introduce new ideas will be met on all sides by conformities and mental apathy. Obviously it is not essential that a dramatist should wish to be unpopular, but neither is it essential that he should wish to be popular. His efforts, his creative work are above such considerations. Either this theatre will always remain unpopular, will never be recognised and so will never exist as theatre or it will in time, naturally and by the force of circumstances, become popular and generally recognised.

Today everyone understands the elementary laws of physics

or geometry, which must certainly have been at first only understood by learned men who never thought of offering the public popular geometry or physics. They did not express the truth of a certain narrow caste but truths which were undeniably objective. The question of the similarities which may exist between science and art does not fall within my province.

We all know that the differences between these two domains of the mind are far greater than the similarities. However, each new author seeks to fight in the name of truth. Boileau wished to express truth. In his Preface to *Cromwell*, Victor Hugo considered that Romantic Art rather than Classical contained more truth and was more complex. The aim of Realism and Naturalism was also to extend the realms of reality or reveal new and still unknown aspects of it. Symbolism and later Surrealism were further attempts to reveal and express hidden realities.

The question then is simply for an author to discover truths and to state them. And the manner of stating them is naturally unfamiliar for this statement itself is the truth for him. He can only speak it for himself. It is by speaking it for himself that he speaks it for others. Not the other way round.

If I want to write popular drama at any price, I run the risk of imparting truths which have not been discovered by myself, but which have already been imparted to me by others and which I would only be passing on at second hand. The artist is not a pedagogue, neither is he a demagogue. Dramatic creation satisfies a mental need, this need must be sufficient in itself. A tree is a tree, it does not need my permission to be a tree, the tree is not faced with the problem of being a certain kind of tree in order to be recognised as a tree. It does not make itself explicit. It exists and is made manifest by its very existence.

It does not seek to make itself understood. It does not assume a more understandable form; otherwise it would no longer be a tree but only the explanation of a tree. In the same way, a work of art is sufficient in itself and I can easily imagine drama without a public. The public will come by itself, and will recognise this theatre as it recognises a tree as a tree.

The songs of Béranger were far more popular than the poems of Rimbaud, who was quite incomprehensible in his day. Should one for that reason exclude Rimbaud's poetry? Eugène Sue was extremely popular. Proust was not. He was not understood. He did not speak to everyone. He simply contributed his kind of truth towards the development of literature and the mind. Should one debar Proust and recommend Sue? Today it is Proust who offers a wealth of truth, it is Eugène Sue who seems empty. How fortunate that the authorities did not forbid Proust to write in Proustian language!

A creative idea can only be expressed by a means of expression which is suited to it, so much so that idea and means of expression are one and the same.

There is popular theatre and popular theatre. We think, erroneously, that popular theatre must be theatre for those who are lacking in intellect: but there is the kind which is intended to instruct, a theatre for our edification, elementary (and not primitive, which is not the same thing), the tool of a political creed, of some ideology of which it is the duplicate — a useless and 'conformist' repetition.

A work of art and a dramatic work too, therefore, must be a primary instinct, profound or vast according to the talent or genius of the artist, but a truly primary instinct which owes nothing to anything but itself. But in order that it may rise up and take shape, one must let the imagination run free above external and secondary considerations such as those of its future, its popularity or its need to express an ideology. In this flowering of the imagination, meanings emerge by themselves and they are eloquent for some and less so for others. For my part I cannot understand how anyone can have the ambition to speak for everybody, to possess the unanimous support of the public while, within one class of people for instance, some prefer strawberries, others cheese, some prefer aspirin for their headaches, others bismuth for their stomach-aches. In any case, I don't worry about the support of the public. Or perhaps I do, but only when the play has been written and I am considering the question of how to place it. Support comes or doesn't come, quite naturally. It is quite certain that one can never speak for everybody. At the most, one can speak on behalf of a large majority and in this case one can only produce demagogic or ready-made drama. If you wish to speak to everybody, you will really speak to no-one: the things which interest everybody in general have very little interest for each man in particular. Besides which, a creative work of art is, by its very novelty, aggressive, spontaneously aggressive; it strikes out at the public, against the vast majority; it rouses indignation by its nonconformity which is, in itself, a form of indignation. This is inevitable, for it does not keep to the beaten track but opens up a new one, cutting across country, alone. This is the sense in which a work of art is unpopular, as as I have already said. But new art is only apparently unpopular; it is not so in essence, it is unpopular only because of its unfamiliarity. The so-called popular theatre is actually far more unpopular. It is a theatre which is arrogantly imposed throughout by a ruling aristocracy, a special class of initiates who know or think they know in advance what the public needs. They even say to the public: 'You must only need what we want you to need and you must only think in the way we think.' Paradoxically, the free work of art, by its individualistic character, despite its unusual appearance, alone springs from men's hearts, through a man's heart; it is the only thing which really expresses the people.

It is said that the theatre is in danger and in a critical state. This is due to many reasons. Very soon dramatists will be made apostles of all kinds of theologies, they will not be free, they will be told only to defend, attack or praise this or that. If they are not apostles, then they are pedants. Elsewhere the theatre is the prisoner not of ideologies but conventions, taboos, hardened mental habits, fixations. When the theatre could be the place of the greatest freedom, of the wildest imaginings, it has become that of the greatest constraint, of a rigid and set system of conventions which may be called 'realist' or otherwise. We are afraid of too much humour, (and humour is freedom). We are afraid of freedom of thought, of a play that is too tragic or too despairing. Optimism and hope are compulsory under pain of death. And what is sometimes labelled the absurd is only the denunciation of the ridiculous nature of a language empty of substance, sterile, made up of clichés and slogans; of theatre-that-is-known-in-advance. I personally would like to bring a tortoise onto the stage, turn it into a racehorse, then into a hat, a song, a dragoon and a fountain of water. One can dare anything in the theatre and it is the place where one dares the least.

I want no other limits than the technical limits of the stage machinery. People will say that my plays are music-hall or circus. So much the better: let's bring in the circus! One can accuse the dramatist of being arbitrary, but the theatre is the place where one can be arbitrary. As a matter of fact, it is not arbitrary. The imagination is not arbitrary, it is revealing. Without the guarantee of total freedom, the dramatist will never be himself, he will say nothing except what has already been formulated: my own intention was not to recognise any laws except those of my imagination, and since the imagination has laws this is a further proof that finally it is not arbitrary.

It has been said that what distinguishes man from the other animals is that he is the animal that laughs; he is above all else the animal that creates. He introduces into the world things which were not there before: temples and rabbit-hutches, wheelbarrows, locomotives, symphonies, poems, cathedrals and cigarettes. The usefulness of all these things is often only a pretext. What is the use of existing? — To exist. What is the use of a flower? — To be a flower. Of what use is a temple or a cathedral? To house the faithful? I doubt it, since the temples are no longer used and we still admire them. They serve to reveal to us the laws of architecture, and perhaps of universal construction, which are apparently reflected in our mind since the mind discovers these laws within itself. But the theatre is dying for lack of courage. We seem no longer to realise that a world we invent cannot be false. It can only be false if I want to fabricate a truth and imitate truth, for in so doing I fabricate a false truth. I am conscious of being true when I invent and imagine. Nothing is clearer or more 'logical' than something constructed by the imagination. I could even go so far as to say that to me it is the world that seems irrational, that is growing irrational and baffles my understanding. The laws to which I try continually to adapt and submit it, I find in my own mind. But this again lies outside our province.

When an author writes something, a play for instance, he has, as I have said, the clear or confused impression that he is fighting a battle, that if he has something to say, it is because others have not said that thing properly, or that they no longer know how to say it. He wishes to say something new, otherwise why would he write? To say what he has to say, to impose his world is itself the battle. A tree in order to grow must overcome the resistance of matter. For an author, this matter is the already-done, the already-said. He writes not for or against something but in spite of something. In this sense, each artist is to varying degrees and according to his powers, a rebel. If he copies, if he reproduces, if he exemplifies, he is nothing. It therefore seems that a poet is fighting against a tradition — but in most cases involuntarily, by the mere fact of his existence.

To the extent that a poet feels that the language no longer corresponds to reality, no longer expresses a truth, he must endeavour to capture reality, to express it better, in a way that is more pungent, more eloquent, clearer, more apt and precise. By this means, he overtakes and modernises a living tradition which had got lost. An avant-garde dramatist can feel, and in any case this is his wish, that he is making a better attempt than others around him. He is making a real attempt to return to the source. But what source? That of the Theatre. A return to an inner ideal of the theatre; for it is in oneself that one discovers the deep and permanent foundations of theatre.

Pascal discovered within himself the principles of geometry, Mozart as a child discovered in himself the rudiments of his music. Very few artists of course can measure up to the stature of these two giants. Nevertheless, it seems certain to me that one hasn't got what is so aptly called 'theatre in the blood' if one cannot reinvent a little oneself. I am also quite certain that if all libraries were swallowed up in some great cataclysm together with all museums, those who escaped would sooner or later rediscover for themselves painting, music and theatre which, like bodily functions, are as natural, necessary and instinctive as breathing. He who does not possess even to a slight degree the functions of drama, is not a man of the theatre. To discover it one must perhaps have a certain ignorance, a certain naïvety, a boldness that springs from this naïvety but a naïvety that is not simplicity of mind, and an ignorance that does not rule out knowledge but assimilates and rejuvenates it. A work of art is not devoid of ideas. Since it is life or the expression of life, ideas are emanated from it: the work of art does not emanate from an ideology. The new dramatist is one who, contradictorily, endeavours to overtake what is most ancient: new language and subject matter in a dramatic structure which aims at being clearer, more stripped of inessentials and more purely theatrical; the rejection of traditionalism to rediscover tradition; a synthesis of knowledge and invention, of the real and the imaginary, of the particular and the universal or as they say now, of the individual and the collective; the expression, over and above classes, of that which transcends them. By expressing my deepest obsessions, I express my deepest humanity. I become one with all others, spontaneously, over and above all the barriers of caste and different psychologies. I express my solitude and become one with all other solitudes; my joy at existing or my surprise at being are those of every-one even if, for the moment, everyone refuses to recognise it. A play such as *The Quare Fellow* by the Irish writer, Brendan Behan, was the fruit of his own experience: prison. Neverthe-less I feel concerned, for this prison becomes all prisons, it becomes the world and all its classes of people. Inside this

English prison there are of course prisoners and there are warders. That is: slaves and masters, the rulers and the ruled. They are all enclosed within the same walls. The prisoners hate their warders, the warders scorn their prisoners. But the prisoners also loathe one another, and neither do the warders agree amongst themselves. If there were just the simple conflict between the warders on the one hand and the prisoners on the other; if the play were limited to this obvious conflict, there would be nothing new, profound or revealing, but a coarse and crudely sketched reality. But this play shows that reality is far more complex. A man in this prison is to be executed. The condemned man does not appear on the stage. He is however present in our consciousness and continually haunts us. He has the leading role. Or rather death has the leading role. Warders and prisoners feel together this presence of death. The play's deep humanity dwells in the terrible communion of this haunting thought, this agony which is shared by all, transcending the categories of warder and prisoner. It is a communion beyond differences, an almost unconscious feeling of fellowship of which the dramatist makes us conscious. The common identity of all men is revealed to us. This helps to draw all enemy camps together. Indeed, the prisoners and warders suddenly appear to us as mortals, united and governed by the same problem, which surpasses all others. Here is popular theatre indeed, one of communion in the same agony. It is an old play, for it deals with a fundamental and age-old problem. It is a new and localised play, for it deals with a prison at a certain moment in time in a particular country.

At the beginning of this century and in the 1920's in particular, a vast universal avant-garde movement was felt in all domains of the mind and human activity. An overthrowing of our mental habits. Modern painting from Klee to Picasso, from Matisse to Mondrian, from Cubism to Abstractionism expresses this overthrow, this revolution. It emerged in music and films and it affected architecture. Philosophy and psychology were transformed. Science (but I am not competent to speak on this subject) gave us a new vision of the world. A new style emerged and continues to emerge. An age is distinguished by its unity of style, a synthesis of various styles and so there are obvious similarities between architecture and poetry, mathematics and music. There is an essential unity between the Palace of Versailles and Cartesian thought, for instance. Literature and drama from André Breton to Maïakovski, from Marinetti to Tristan Tzara or Apollinaire, from the Expressionist drama to Surrealism, down to the most recent novels by Faulkner and Dos Passos and quite recently those of Nathalie Sarraute and Michel Butor, have all shared in this surge of new life. But all literature did not follow this movement and in the theatre it seems to have been arrested in 1930. The theatre is the most behindhand. The avant-garde was halted in the theatre if not in literature. Wars, revolutions, Nazism and other forms of tyranny, dogmatism, and in some countries bourgeois inertia too, have prevented it developing for the moment. But it must be resumed. I myself hope to be one of the modest artisans trying to restart this movement. Indeed, this abandoned avant-garde movement has not been outstripped but buried by the reactionary return of old dramatic formulas that sometimes dare to pretend they are new ones. The theatre is not of our age: it manifests a dated psychology, the light comedy style, bourgeois prudence and a realism which refuses to be called conventional but which really is, a submission to dogmatism which is a menace to the artist.

The young generation of French film production is far more advanced than that of the theatre. Young film producers have been trained in film libraries and film clubs. This is where they have received their education. There they have seen art films; the great classics of the cinema, avant-garde films uncommercial and non-popular, many of which have never been shown in big cinemas or have only been shown for a short time because of their uncommercial nature.

Although it is far more difficult for the theatre, it also needs these places for experiment, these laboratories protected from the superficiality of the general public. A danger in some countries, and still a necessary evil unfortunately, is the manager. He is a tyrant in this domain. The theatre must show a profit; to do so all boldness and creativeness must be eliminated so as not to upset anyone. A manager once asked me to change everything in my plays and make them comprehensible. I asked him by what right he interfered with matters of dramatic construction which should only concern myself and my producer: for it seemed to me that to pay money to put on the play was not sufficient reason to dictate conditions and alter my work. He replied that he represented the public. I replied that we had to wage war against the public and against him, the manager. To wage war against him or else ignore him.

We need a liberal State, befriending thought and art, believing in their necessity and the necessity for laboratories. Before an invention or a scientific theory is made known, it has been long prepared, tested out and thought out in the laboratories. I claim that dramatists should have the same opportunities as scientists for making experiments. One cannot say that a scientific discovery is. for that reason, unpopular. I do not think the realities of the mind, welling up from the deepest part of my being, are unpopular. To have a public is not always to be popular. The aristocracy of poets is not a false aristocracy like an aristocracy of caste.

In France we have some exciting new dramatists: Jean Genet, Beckett, Vauthier, Pichette, Schehadé, Audiberti, Ghelderode, Adamov, Georges Neveux, who carry on the tradition, while opposing it, of Giraudoux, Anouilh, Jean-Jacques Bernard and many others. They are only points of departure for a possible development of a free and living theatre.

For the avant-garde stands for freedom.

> (June 1959, Helsinki — September 1959,
> *Théâtre dans le Monde*, from which this
> translation is taken.)

STILL ABOUT AVANT-GARDE THEATRE

What is meant by '*avant-garde* theatre'? Deliberate or not, great confusion has arisen round these words, mainly owing to prejudice. The expression itself is confusing and the idea that avant-garde theatre is 'ridiculous' might even be caused merely by faulty definition. A critic in one of the foreign countries where I have been lucky enough to see my plays acted — favourable, moreover, to my work — still wondered whether this kind of theatre was not after all just a transition, a stage in the development of drama. So that is what avant-garde means: a kind of drama that opens the way to another kind of drama, which will be definitive. But nothing is definitive, everything is just a stage in development, our very lives are essentially transitory: everything is, at one and the same time, the culmination of one thing and the announcement of something else. So one can say that the French theatre of the seventeenth century prepares the way for Romantic drama (which is not worth much anyway in France) and that Racine and Corneille are the advance guard of the theatre of Victor Hugo, who himself blazed the trail for what came after and rejected him.

And again: the mechanism governing forward and rear positions is far more complicated than the blinkered dialecticians imagine. There are some productive 'avant-garde' movements which arise from opposition to the achievements of preceding generations or, on the other hand, others which are encouraged or facilitated by a reappraisal of sources, of old and forgotten works. Shakespeare is always far more contemporary than Victor Hugo (cited above); Pirandello far more 'avant-garde' than Roger Ferdinand; Büchner infinitely more poignant and alive than, for example, Bertholt Brecht and his imitators in Paris.

And this is where matters seem to become clearer: in reality, the avant-garde does not exist; or rather it is quite different from what it is thought to be.

As the avant-garde is, we all agree, revolutionary, it has always been and still is, like most revolutionary movements, a turning back, a reappraisal. The change is only apparent: this 'apparentness' is of enormous importance, for it is this that allows (by presenting something new and yet going beyond it) reassessment and restoration of something permanent. For example: the political upheavals that appear at moments when a regime is worn out and 'liberalised' — when the structure has weakened to such a point that collapse is anyway imminent, ready to take place, as one might say, unaided — prepare and allow for a strengthening and reconstitution of the social structure according to an archetypal and changeless model: there is a real change on the personal plane, obviously, on the level of superficial conditions, in idiom: that is to say things — identical in essence — assume different names, without modifying the deeper reality or the fundamental pattern of society.

What has really happened? Simply this: authority (which had been relaxed) has tightened up, 'order' is re-established, tyranny clamps down again on freedom, the leaders of the state recover their taste and vocation for power with a quiet conscience, for they feel themselves to be invested with a kind of 'God's Grace', with an alibi provided by a firm and reliable ideological justification for the cynicism inseparable from power. And there we have the basic hierarchical social structure, clearly reaffirmed and reconstituted, with the king (the political leaders) upheld by dogma and the church (the ideologists, the writers, the artists, the journalists, the propagandists, all back in obedience) and either supported or suffered by the majority—the people (the believers, the faithful or the passive) who are no longer capable of insurrection.

Almost the same thing happens with artistic revolutions, when there is really an attempt at revolution, or a revolutionary experiment coming from the avant-garde. This happens inevitably, of its own accord as you might say, at a moment when certain modes of expression have become exhausted and worn out, when they have deteriorated, when they have wandered too far from some forgotten model. Thus, in painting, the moderns have been able to *rediscover* in the painters we call 'primitives' forms that are pure and permanent, the basic laws that govern their art. And this rediscovery, dictated by the history of art where forms and models lose their power — has been made possible thanks to an art, an *idiom* that springs from a reality lying outside history.

It is indeed in the union between the historical and the unhistorical, the topical and the untopical (that is to say the permanent) that we can seek this changeless basic material which can also succeed in finding, instinctively, in ourselves: without it, any work of art is valueless, it keeps everything alive. So finally I maintain quite fearlessly that the true avant-garde or revolutionary art is that which, boldly setting its face against its own times, looks as if it is *untopical*. By casting off all claim to topicality, it reveals its links with this universal basic material we have already spoken of, and being universal it may be considered classical; but it should be understood that this classicism must be rediscovered by passing through and going beyond the new elements that should permeate this kind of art. Any attempt to return to some sort of 'historical' classicism by turning one's back on what is new would only encourage the development of an outdated and academic style. For example: *Endgame* by Beckett, a so-called avant-garde play is far closer to the lamentations of *Job*, the tragedies of Sophocles or Shakespeare, than to the tawdry drama known as committed or boulevard theatre. Topical drama does not last (by definition) and it does not last for the good reason that people are not truly profoundly interested in it.

It is also worth noting that social changes are not always related to artistic revolution. Or rather: when the mystique of a revolution becomes a regime, it returns to artistic forms (and so to a mentality) that are outmoded, with the result that the new realism is bound up with the mental clichés we call bourgeois and reactionary. Conventionalism repeats itself and the bewhiskered academic portraits of the new reaction are — stylistically — no different from the academic portraits, with or without whiskers, of the bourgeois period which did not understand Cézanne. So we can say, somewhat paradoxically perhaps, *that it is the 'historical' which is moribund, and the non-historical which remains alive.*

Chekov in his drama shows us dying men in a particular dying society; the destruction, as time runs out and gnaws away, of the men of a certain period; Proust too had done this in his novels — and so had Gustave Flaubert in *L'Éducation sentimentale*, although he showed as a background to his characters not a declining but a rising society. So it is not the collapse or the break-up or the erosion of a social system which is the principal theme, the *truth* of these works: but man eroded by time, his destruction seen at a certain historical moment but true for *all* history; we are *all* murdered by time.

I mistrust pacifist plays, which seem to be showing us that it is war that destroys mankind and that we only die in wartime. This is more or less what one young critic seemed to be saying, obstinately dogmatic, when commenting on *Mother Courage*.

More of us die in wartime: topical truth. We die: permanent truth, not topical yet always topical, it concerns everybody, and so it also concerns people not involved in war: Beckett's *Endgame* is more true, more universal, than Schehadé's *Histoire de Vasco* (which in no way prevents this play from having high poetic qualities).

Since at first sight 'what concerns us all fundamentally' is curiously less accessible than what concerns only some people or what concerns us less — it is obvious that avant-garde plays, whose aim is (I apologize for being so insistent) to rediscover and make known a forgotten truth — and to reintegrate it, in an untopical way, into what is topical — it is obvious that when these works appear they cannot help being misunderstood by the majority of people. So they are not 'popular'. This in no way invalidates them. The plainest realities are discovered by the poet in silence and solitude. The philosopher too, in the silence of his library, discovers truths difficult to communicate: how long did it take for Karl Marx himself to be understood, and even now can *everyone* understand him? He is not 'popular'. How many people have succeeded in assimilating Einstein? The fact that only a few people are capable of a clear understanding of the theories of modern physicists does not make me doubt their validity; and this truth that they have discovered is neither invention nor subjective vision, but objective reality, outside time, eternal, and the scientific mind has only just touched the fringe of it. Where we are concerned with an unchanging truth, all we ever do is approach, move away and then draw closer again.

There also exists — as we are meant to be talking about the theatre — a dramatic idiom, a theatrical method of approach, a trail to blaze, if we are to reach a reality that has objective existence: and this trail to blaze (or path to find again) cannot be other than one belonging to the theatre, which will lead to a reality that can only be revealed theatrically. It is what we might agree to call laboratory research.

There is no reason why there should not be drama for *the people* (I am not quite sure who the people are, unless it is the majority, the non-specialists), boulevard theatre, a theatre of propaganda and instruction, composed in some conventional idiom: this is popularised theatre. We must not for this reason prevent the other kind of theatre from continuing its work: a drama of research, laboratory drama, the avant-garde. If it is not taken up by a large public, this in no way means that it is not of vital importance to our minds, as necessary as artistic, literary or scientific research. We do not always know *what use it is* — but as it fulfills a mental requirement, it is clearly quite indispensable. If such drama has an audience of 50 people every evening (and it can have that number) the need for it is proved. This kind of theatre is in danger. Politics, apathy, malice and jealousy are unfortunately, a dangerous threat on every side to such writers as Beckett, Vauthier, Schehadé, Weingarten and others as well as to their supporters.

(*Arts*, January 1958.)

REMARKS ON MY THEATRE AND ON THE
REMARKS OF OTHERS

When we hear people talking about a work of literature, music, drama or the plastic arts, it is quite natural that we should wish to examine it more closely and find out what is being said about this new topic of conversation. The author is asked to let us into the secret of what he thinks about his own work. After the work has been exhibited, acted or published, is easy to know what the critics think about it, and so *their* writings are devoured; and then the author is approached again and asked to say what *he* thinks about what people think about his work and about himself. It goes without saying that there is very often a contradiction between the author's statements and the opinions of the critics, and so they are approached in turn and asked for *their* opinion about what they think about what the author thinks about what they themselves think. And so on, *ad infinitum:* passionate argument arises out of all this; some are for, some are against; there will be learned lectures to establish that the work supports this or that theory, this or that philosophy, or rather that it would appear to have tendencies that refute them; and so it comes about that one has to be for or against the work, or against or for it, according to whether one does or does not subscribe to the theory in question, . . . or a theory not in question, for some may claim that it is *that* theory rather than *this* theory which the work — according, of course, to what is said about it — would seem to be defending.

The voice of the work itself can no longer be heard through the din of debate; while all kinds of points of view are being developed, it is always the work itself that is lost sight of. It appears to be of little further use to come to terms with the work itself since one forms one's opinion of it according to the opinions of others, and when, after all, judgment *is* sometimes passed on something, it is these *opinions* that are judged, rejected or adopted.

Perhaps a work of art really *is* only what is thought about it. But rather than think about it through the minds of others, would it not be better to think about the work itself and pay no attention to the prohibitions, warnings and encouragements so prodigally bestowed on it?

It sometimes happens that I am visited by people interested in my drama, or by the disturbance created round it. So recently I welcomed three young intellectuals, intelligent and well-informed, who also wanted to know what I thought about my own work. They knew everything that had been said about it, favourable or unfavourable; the first one agreed with the opinions of the critics in my favour, the second one let me understand in friendly fashion that he agreed with the attitude taken up by my enemies; whereas the third one could not quite agree with either and tried lucidly and objectively to decide between them. During this conversation I came to realise that my three visitors knew little about my plays, either from the printed page or on the stage. They were therefore talking round their subject, indifferent to the thing itself, and this in their opinion was quite normal, for it is not the thing itself, only its general repercussion, that matters. This is an idea that can be defended, although one may remark that it is not unusual for the public's reactions to be overtly or discreetly perverted or manipulated. Has not one of the masters of contemporary thought declared — clumsily moreover, if in fashionable terms — that it was necessary to 'mystify

in order to demystify'? At what precise moment does demystification take over from this mystification, which
would thus be, if one might say, an honest mystification,
practised in good faith? And is the demystifier not himself
mystified? Who can say, who is qualified to judge? One
needs to be very sure of oneself to claim the ability to lead
people by the nose along the path of truth and goodness, and
still more sure to claim one knows what this path, this goodness or this truth is, even if the latter is simply relative and
historical. Nowadays there are many dogmas, many dogmatic
thinkers: could it be that these dogmatic doctrines now provide the framework for our subjective responses?

I will not suggest that nowadays we do not think. But we
think about what a few leading thinkers give us to think about,
we think about what *they* think, if we do not think exactly
what they think, repeating or paraphrasing their thoughts. In
any case, it is clear that three or four thinkers have taken the
initiative in thought and chosen their own weapons and
battleground; and the thousands of other thinkers who
believe they think thrash about in the intellectual nets cast by
the three others, trapped by the terms in which the latter
force them to consider the problem. The problem imposed
upon them may have its importance. But there are also other
problems, other aspects of reality and the world: and the
least we can say of our leading thinkers is that they restrict us to
their own more or less doctrinaire subjective approach, which
conceals from us, like a screen, the infinitely varied points of
view possible to the human spirit. But to think for oneself, to
discover problems for oneself is an extremely difficult thing.
It is so much more convenient to find one's nourishment in
predigested foods. We are or have been the pupils of this or

that teacher. And not only has he taught us, he has influenced us by his own way of thinking, his theories, his subjective view of the truth. In short he has 'formed' us. It is chance that has formed us: for if this same chance had sent us to a different school, a different teacher would have fashioned our minds in his own image, and our thinking would doubtless have been of a different kind. I am certainly not suggesting we should reject the basic ideas given to us, or pour scorn on the opinions and solutions chosen by others: anyhow, this is not possible: but we should think out for ourselves the problems we are asked to think about and the terms in which we are asked to think, to try and discover what particular subjective elements there are in ideas presented to us as objective or generally accepted; we should be on our guard and remain free to put our own examiners through our own examination; and only when this has been done accept or reject their point of view. I believe it is better to think clumsily, inadequately, as best one may, than to rattle off the current slogans, good, bad or indifferent. A man, even a foolish one, is still worth more than a wise and intelligent donkey; my own little discoveries and platitudes have more value and contain more truth for me than the meaning a parrot can find in the brilliant or subtle aphorisms he can do no more than repeat.

Young people, chiefly, and the masses are solicited on every side. Politicians are out for votes and leaders of thought in search of disciples: a master philosopher preaching in the desert would be too ridiculous; they want to have an effect on other people, they want to possess them, they want a following, they want to force other people to support them, whereas a good teacher, instead of imposing his ideas, enthusiasms or personality on other people, should try to encourage and

c

develop the personality of others. It is, I know, very difficult to decide to what extent the ideology of an ideologist is or is not the result of a desire for self-assertion and the pursuit of personal power; for this very reason we must be even more vigilant.

I am wondering if what I have been saying does not go beyond the limits of this talk. We shall see in a moment. I have not come here to indoctrinate you: though you may answer that it is still preaching to maintain that one must not preach. If this is so, it is just too bad, it is the only kind of preaching I will allow myself; but rather than a sermon this is a warning, a friendly appeal for vigilance, and I admit it can be turned against me. This little talk should not just be called 'Remarks on my Theatre', for I hope instead it will contain 'Remarks on the Remarks of others about my Theatre'.

And so the learned doctors wish to be obeyed. They are furious if they are disobeyed. They do not like you to be what you are, they would rather you were what *they* want you to be. They want you to play their game, accept their politics and become their tool. And if this fails they would rather wipe you out, unless they can manage to prove that you are still what they want you to be, even if you are not.

For a dramatist like myself, for example, who are these doctors? Well, they are the learned, the less learned and the not learned at all. That is to say, those 'engaged' or enraged critics who positively refuse to accept you as you are: some because of their own theories, some because of their fixed mental habits, and others because of their temperament or their allergies, in other words for subjective reasons that are less complex and more fanciful. But whatever their reasons they are all more or less learned doctors, even if really they are not. It is quite obvious that you only judge others through your own personality or principles, even if it is desirable that you should make a supreme effort to accept the other person, to accept him as he is. That is the first rule of a liberalism that to-day has gone out of fashion, even with liberal-minded people.

However, this is not exactly relevant, or rather it is as relevant as it is to any sectarianism that limits the humanity of the sectarians themselves as well as the intellectual horizon of all of us, which they are bent on narrowing or obstructing. The real problem is to know what credit we can give to the incoherent subjectivity of these critics, setting up emotional contradictions that conflict with their own standards or their immediate reactions and confuse various levels of judgement. We must also consider, although this is perhaps less important, the great variety of opinion, which is after all embarrassing for an author seeking advice from criticism as well as for theatregoers looking for guidance in their choice of plays to see.

It is not primarily this variety of opinions which is disturbing, even if they are unfavourable to me; on the contrary, general approbation would be very disquieting. Did not Jean Paulhan in his 'A Short Preface to All Criticism' write that 'Blame from the critics nowadays serves a work of art better than praise. If the Marquis de Sade, Baudelaire, Rimbaud, and Lautréamont reach us now with astonishing freshness, it is thanks to a number of disparaging or defamatory comments: from Jules Janin, Brunetière, Maurras, France, Faguet and Gourmont. A good slating preserves an author better than alcohol preserves fruit. It would seem as though we were in fact more responsive — far more responsive than to that obvious aspect of criticism which consists of explanation, elaboration and the rest — to that secret element (secret, supposedly, because there is little evidence for it) which first leads a critic to admit that an author is worth examining, contesting and demolishing . . .' Especially demolishing. True, of course, but what an author finds so unpleasant is when they do not want to listen to him attentively before taking up a position, and when the positions held are held dishonestly: the very least we may ask of a critic is objectivity within his own subjective limits, and by that I mean good faith.

In England two or three dramatic critics set the tone. They are the most enlightened, the most efficient critics, with the greatest influence over the intellectuals and lovers of the theatre. They are the theatrical guides for the more informed section of the audience. One of them has an artistic and literary background. He has a feeling for literature, which is becoming more and more rare in our time, he is free and open-minded and accepts that there can be many different trends. The other critic is a stylist who toys with Marx, he is younger, with a slightly more philosophical background, formerly at Oxford, much concerned with ideologies and very much aware of intellectual fashions. Both of these London critics have done me the honour of writing about my drama and making it better-known, since the first performances of my early plays in English, of *Les Chaises*, for example.

Several months after the appearance of a very laudatory article on the play by the younger of the two critics, I met him at a friend's house. I expressed my thanks and we started a conversation during which he suddenly announced that I could, if I wanted, be the greatest writer in the theatre to-day: 'Nothing would please me more', I said, excitedly, 'tell me the recipe at once!'

'It's very easy', he answered, 'we are only waiting for you to deliver us a message. Up to now your plays do not have the message we were hoping from you. Be a Marxist, be Brechtian!'

In reply I answered that someone had already brought this message: it was well-known, welcomed by some, repudiated by others, but in any case the problem had now been stated; if I did the same I should only be restating it, and as I should have nothing new to say I would certainly not become, as he suggested, 'the greatest dramatist in the theatre of our time'.

This critic could not forgive me. And he showed it. A few months later, at the revival of the same play, *Les Chaises*, he wrote a fairly long article, in which he was bent on proving that he had been mistaken the first time in praising the play so highly and that he had finally realised it could not stand up to a second visit. Almost the same thing happened to me here in Paris with a young critic not so much learned as dogmatic. The latter had asked me if I agreed with what he had written about some of my early plays, which he considered to be a criticism of *la petite bourgeoisie*. I replied that I was only partly in agreement with his statements. Indeed, there probably was in my plays some criticism of the *petite bourgeoisie*, but the *petite bourgeoisie* I had in mind was not a class belonging to any particular society, for the *petit bourgeois* was for me a type of being that exists in all societies, whether they be called revolutionary or reactionary; for me the *petit bourgeois* is just a man of slogans, who no longer thinks for himself but repeats the truths that others have imposed upon him, ready-made and therefore lifeless. In short the *petit bourgeois* is a manipulated man. I even thought this young anti-bourgeois critic might well be *petit bourgeois* himself. From that day on this critic's articles on the same plays became unfavourable, and yet I had not changed a single line in these texts. I had merely refused point blank to agree with his interpretation; I had refused to play his game. This same critic had written a long article about my plays and those of another dramatist in an important weekly magazine, illustrated by photos of the two of us right in the middle of the page. What these two dramatists have written up to date, said the critic, is very good, very useful: they have 'destroyed' a certain theatrical idiom, now they must reconstruct it; they have criticised, they have rejected, now they must take a positive line. What positive line? The line our doctor-critic wanted us to take, of course. I did not follow the itinerary traced out for me by this doctor. The other writer did: he has been widely acclaimed along the primrose path; but I was reproached and excommunicated, hot coals were heaped upon my head by him and his friends, for only one kind of drama is permissible to them, co-existence is a word they do not understand.

If I had been artful, I could, by accepting his interpretation of my first plays, at least verbally, have saved them in the eyes of this critic. Some authors like to be appreciated by everyone, even at the price of misunderstanding. My lack of diplomacy has given some doctor-critics reason for doubt about my early plays too. In fact they have been depreciated retrospectively: not only does this give one terrible doubts about the objectivity of these critics, but even worse it calls into question the possibility of criticism at all, when critics can maintain two contradictory opinions about the same work at the same or almost the same time.

And this is still more irritating or perturbing when, if the critic is sufficiently ingenious, each separate opinion seems to account for the work equally well, seems to explain it perfectly, and satisfies the mind of anyone who follows that critic. Others, before me, have wondered whether criticism is really possible. The same doubts could be raised about the validity of all ideologies. If according to this or that ideological standard you can maintain that a work of art, an event, a political or economic system, history or the human condition, means one thing or another quite indiscriminately; if several different interpretations seem to explain and account for all the facts according to a given system, without major internal contradiction, and all of them seem valid; and if one can discover, and one always does if one wants to, that these historical facts confirm and bring grist to this ideological mill as well as that one, it may prove that no ideology is binding, that it depends on nothing but points of view and personal choice, and has no objective truth. That leaves us with science. And artistic creation — which, even if it has to be interpreted subjectively, as a kind of monument, an autonomous structure or universe, assumes objective reality.

'To come back to our sheep', and by that I mean: our critics, I am going to quote another case of incoherence on the part of one of my literary judges. It concerns a member of the Académie Française, a perfect example of the man of letters, a humanist and an impressionist. Naturally an impressionist has a greater right to incoherence than a man who claims to observe well-established ideological criteria. The incoherence of the dramatic critic in question was, however, too serious not to be shocking. His impressionism, or rather his impressions, were easy to forecast when he was going to have to criticise a class of work which one knew was written in a style to which he was accustomed: classical plays or so-called 'boulevard' plays, or even those written in a different but already accepted style. Any work that was not quite like the models he already knew, any play of this kind, whether the younger or more daring critics found it good or bad, was incomprehensible to him, it escaped him. A few years ago, when my first play, *La Cantatrice Chauve*, was first performed, he said 'that the most it deserved was a shrug of the shoulders'. Later on, when he had seen the performance of another play, *Les Chaises*, at the *Studio des Champs-Elysées*, he wrote that it reminded him, though of course it was much worse, of one of Anatole France's short stories, but without fantasy, invention or wit. He closed his article by saying that he could not understand how anything so flat could have been written by the author, 'full of fantasy and humour', of the 'brilliant' *Cantatrice Chauve*. At the opening of almost every one of my plays he lamented the dazzling author of the previous one. Last year, at the *Théâtre Récamier*, *Tueur sans gages* was performed. He dismissed it in a long. stylish, well-argued and scathing article, saying that the play was anti-theatrical, inaudible, unreadable and incomprehensible. He ended his attack with the declaration that he could not be accused of prejudice, as he had loved and defended *La Cantatrice Chauve*, *La Leçon* and *Les Chaises* when they first appeared. He had, it is true, written a rather favourable review of *Victimes du devoir* in 1953. Three weeks after the first night of *Tueur sans gages*, we gave this play again. with Jacques Mauclair. This time we were sure we would have a good review for *Victimes du devoir*, since our academician had only to refer to what he himself had already written about it: wrong again! Of course this critic could not avoid admitting that he had written what he had written. Deliberately or not, he found a subterfuge by which to justify his bad review. The actors, he said, shouted too much, they were not as good as the actors who had played the same play for the first time four years before. And yet, when we revived it, we had the same actors as before and the same producer.

And it was still this same academician who, when the first of Pirandello's plays to be put on in France was performed just after the First World War, dismissed the author as a complete fraud who would never be heard of again. And yet we can hardly doubt the sincerity of a critic like this who frankly stated to a journalist: 'I have never been wrong'. And the same critic again wrote about *Les Chaises:* 'It is no good at all, just desultory conversation', — which did not stop him maintaining at a later date, when writing of another play, which he thought detestable, that he was all the more surprised 'as he had liked *Les Chaises* so much'.

But I am growing so used to this that it now seems quite in in order to see myself manhandled over my new play by unexpected admirers of older plays for the sake of these older plays which they have forgotten they manhandled in just the same way. If a rather naïve author could still nourish the hope of finding friends ready to censure him and seek to draw enlightenment from their criticisms about his own profession, and if he were the author of the play *Rhinocéros*, his mind would be filled with confusion and despair, so utterly at variance have been the opinions about this play, so completely contradictory, more than ever before, not only about its dramatic value and construction, but also about the meaning it could be made to yield, about its significance, its production, and the possible identification of the author with the chief character in the play. In short, some have blamed the author for writing committed drama and conveying a 'message', whereas others have praised

c*

him for the same reasons, and still others have concluded that
there was no message at all, which for some is a good thing and
for others bad!

For one young critic, writing in a new Drama magazine, the
play is no good at all; apparently it represents complete
abdication on the author's part: fortunately, Jean-Louis
Barrault's excellent production and the actors' performances
just manage to save the evening. For another, the play could
have had great power and considerable significance: unfortunately it has been weakened by the producer, — who reduced
the impact of the play. For a very well-known lady critic, the
play had force and vigour, impeccable development, perfect
construction and classical shape; one says it is a masterpiece;
another that it is far from being one (as if every play must be
either a masterpiece or nothing), for he — which means
'me', — knows nothing of the technique of conversation, the
slow-moving curves that advance dramatic action . . ., rhythmical alternation, the use of pauses etc. The provincial critics or
the Paris correspondents of Moroccan or Algerian newspapers
are more precise, more categorical: it is a disgrace, they say, to
present such a stupid and utterly meaningless rag, this lamentable Punch and Judy show, which bored us to death and is
unworthy of the *Théâtre de France* and a company like Jean-
Louis Barrault's etc. . . . I also offer you a taxpayer's opinion,
which is, I am sure, shared by many other taxpayers too: at
one of the first performances of the play he confided to the
lady next to him, before putting it into writing: 'It's terrible to
think this is a State-subsidised theatre and they put on such
things with *our* money! That's what we pay taxes for!'

For some critics, whose complaints were more moderate,
the first part of the play is good: 'the verbal frenzy so beloved

of Ionesco, his compression of time and the savage analysis of
the mechanism of the cliché only really make their impact
during the first part of the play', and as for the rest 'it must not
be concealed that there are long moments of wordy boredom' —
and the production of this first part is excellent: 'for it is swift-
moving and whimsical'. On the other hand, to another critic, a
philosoper, the first act seemed to be a piling-up of ineptitudes,
'although production and acting of the highest quality', he
says, 'nevertheless amused me. But in the middle of the second
act I fell, — and surely others did too, — under a kind of magic
spell. It was as though I had suddenly been transported the
other side of the curtain, as though what had as yet been nothing
but an absurd spectacle had suddenly got inside me and taken
on undeniable meaning and value; and from that moment
until the end I was continuously held and even captivated . . . I
consider it is a play that must absolutely be seen. But naturally
it is good to be prepared to feel somewhat hoaxed or even
irritated by the first part . . . In any case, theatrically, it is a
surprising success, helped moreover by an extraordinarily
ingenious and efficient production . . .' This is not the opinion
of another critic, also a philosopher, who though favourable
to the play as a whole thinks that 'the acting at the Odéon is
brilliant, but neither the atmosphere of this large theatre nor
the production serves the play well. A first act that is too long,
sets that are too complicated and music that is too emphatically
concrete make this play look like a 'great machine' . . . We
would be more aware of its depth, if it were less imposing in
length and breadth'.

This is by no means the opinion of another, who concludes:
'Everyone was wondering whether the Ionesco of the little
theatres would still be himself in the vaster dimensions of the

Théâtre de France. We need not have worried, the author has not changed, he has not tried to adapt himself to new conditions and a new public, he simply brings us proof that he has gained more mastery over his profession as dramatist. His arrival in the subsidised theatres the other evening was triumphant . . .' And yet again, another records: 'Was there really any need to transform a charming and very short story of Ionesco's into an overlong farce with philosophical pretensions? . . . The author who, it seems, had gone in search of the strangeness of the commonplace has unfortunately fallen into the commonplace of strangeness . . . This play, with an idea that could have been amusing . . . was merely a pretext for a rag . . . hardly worth forty minutes' showing; we have been presented with a toothless rhinoceros.' And here is one who maintains: 'The philosophy of the play is brief . . . as in all this author's other plays', and another who claims that 'the philosophical significance of this play is considerable, consequently we have an important work to deal with'. In fact, one critic — who has never exactly spoilt me and who up till then had always called me a fraud, a practical joker, an imbecile, a lunatic and other delightful names — this time finds *Rhinocéros* to be 'a clinical study of conformism, of contamination', which 'shows how movements are born, how fanaticism grows step by step, how dictatorships are formed by unanimous consent and how men contribute to the founding of regimes which will crush them' (and I am myself tempted to believe that this is, as he says, 'the meaning of this farce'): yet this critic does not approve of such plays, for there is 'no earthiness in a drama that is so ideological and so purely demonstrative . . . no life, no soul'; it is, he repeats, 'after all, just a medical and social comment, a laboured intellectual romp'; which does not match the opinion of the philosopher quoted a few moments ago who, on the contrary, you remember, "had been caught and even captivated' and who understands very well that *Rhinocéros* was 'a thumping success' in Germany. 'Not astonishing in Germany, perhaps,' remarks one professor, 'but what is so disappointing about the theatre in France is the crude inventiveness of these rather un-French plays which have brought fame to Beckett, Adamov and Ionesco, would-be metaphysicians whose metaphysics consists in little more than a parody of life translated to the stage in terms of Grand-Guignol', — for indeed, confirms a journalist: 'Beneath its droll and madcap exterior, this drama betrays the disappointing conformism of any *pièce à thèse*' — and in the words of another journalist it is nothing but 'symbolism as puerile as it is old-fashioned'. In addition, another says that the fault of the play 'lies in its total absence of invention, it is monotonous, it flags', although yet another can maintain: 'the author, starting with an idea that is completely gratuitous, swings into his satirical stride with superb nonchalence and a zest enchanted with its own discoveries. This zest is constantly renewed throughout the first two acts of the piece and even intensifies as the plot develops'. Unfortunately, somewhere else we are told that 'this author was only great in the little theatres, *Rhinocéros* is only a vain attempt at epic', for, as we can read in another publication, 'the importance of this author's works has been greatly exaggerated, he has brought us very little; Allais and Jarry went very much further: in short, Ionesco's contribution to the theatre is a very modest one and should be cut down to size'. But this is not the opinion of a student of literary history, who states: 'the rise of Ionesco will soon have lasted ten years. This is not long when one thinks of the far-reaching revolution in ideology and technique demonstrated in his drama, and of the enormous contrast between the incredulous astonishment of his first audiences and the consecration of his present success at the *Odéon*. In 1950 his first producer, Nicolas Bataille, had found great difficulty in discovering the right half-comic half-serious style to suit *La Cantatrice chauve*. The public and the critics were on the whole slow to grasp the implications of this sort of drama', which, as we have just seen in the preceding quotation, are still openly contested. And so on. I confess the attention so kindly bestowed on me, benevolent or malevolent, flatters me, exasperates me in my moments of weakness, troubles and disturbs me, and sometimes I am tempted to believe that the latest article about me is the only one that is right: so after reading it I hurry to the preceding one, which expresses the opposite view, in order not to sink into either fatuity and excessive self-confidence or depression and discouragement, each critic being for me the antidote of the other. This enables me to continue without being thrown off balance by these conflicting pressures which, as they cancel out, are still of service to me: for what possible service can they render, if they do not neutralise each other so as to do me no *dis*service?

I feel I should not fail to point out what in certain critics amounts to a kind of reversal of alliances, provisional I am sure, which took place on the occasion of the first performances of *Rhinocéros:* 'Here it is at last! After the years we've been waiting for it: the day when Ionesco would give up his sterile exercises and become an author worthy of the classics, this day has at last dawned. This time there is no mistake about it: Ionesco writes in French. And his *Rhinocéros* is all the greater for being a work whose meaning we can all understand!'

This is not the opinion of another: 'I can understand why *Rhinocéros* was such a sensation in Germany: it is because this play is essentially Germanic.' Or again: 'At last, for the first time, I have been won over by one of this author's plays.' Whereas for others it is the abomination to end abominations: '*La Leçon* has turned into bad Labiche, *Amédée* into pale Bernstein; a fervent believer in the new theatre has the right to deplore an Ionesco who, having had the genius to discover the strangeness of the commonplace, has fallen into the sermonising symbolism he execrates'.

'Badly written and badly acted, this play is not real Ionesco...' for Ionesco, 'instead of pursuing his own magnificent line, instead of becoming the 'Ionesco squared' we dreamed about, has disfigured the brilliant puppet we knew before by imitating himself.' And yet Ionesco really has 'squared' himself, if we are to believe another article which states textually: 'This play is a fable, it is a myth, it is both Panurge and Prometheus, it is '*Les Chaises*' raised to the power of two: *Rhinocéros* has won the battle'.

I cannot say whether I have won the fight or not, but I notice an inextricable *mêlée* on the battlefield of critics.

One theme doubtless stands out in *Rhinocéros*, since the majority of the critics point to it: disapproval of conformism. Here the reactions are easier to classify. Conformism has a bad press. Everyone finds 'the others' conformist, not himself. To accuse someone of conformism is to accuse him of lacking intelligence or personality: this is not done, it is the chink in everyone's armour, for everyone is scared of being stupid and wonders whether he really is or not.

So when one goes to a play that seems to denounce conformism, one feels disconcerted or annoyed; or on the contrary encouraged and confirmed in an attitude one holds oneself and considers non-conformist: some days after the first night of *Rhinocéros* a critic of traditional or moderately modern art wrote a long article in a weekly paper against 'Rhinoceroses', who in his view are: 'the non-representational painters and lovers of abstract art who are swamping the painting of to-day'; as for him, 'he will never like this painting, he will go on resisting rhinoceritis'. For a well-known dramatic critic of the great bourgeois press rhinoceroses are the authors and partisans of avant-garde theatre (or so-called avant-garde theatre), which he personally, were he the last man in the world, would never accept.

Then those who feel they have been the target concentrate their attack and their reaction is childish: 'The rhinoceroses', explains an eminent non-bourgeois critic to counteract the bourgeois one: 'The rhinoceroses are the Ionescoites'.

The counter-attack becomes more precise when we read: 'I will not capitulate! cries the hero of *Rhinocéros*, faced with the temptations of conformism; for his hero is unfortunately already too late'. Or here is another: 'When the majority of the conformists start approving non-conformism, it stands revealed as only another conformism in disguise . . .' For of course it is clear that 'this kind of drama is comfortable and reassuring, drama that gets at no-one. Judge for yourself . . .' Well then, why all the fuss? Judge for yourself, indeed. And the same critic continues: 'Why in various circumstances have men been led to choose the condition of a rhinoceros? . . . And what if men, by becoming rhinoceroses, wished to escape from a life that is dull and narrow? And what if certain totalitarianisms were to offer a humanism . . . that is more life-giving?' Indeed, that is perhaps what my hero meant:

'Nazism was really one of those life-giving totalitarianisms, very life-giving even and very life-taking.'

When they became aware of my presence on the stage of the *Odéon*, a subsidised theatre, some, the good-natured ones, considered this to be something of a joke on the part of a 'non-conformist' author; others, less good-natured, considered that this was such a serious error as to invalidate all my work. I should like to stress, in passing, that no-one has ever considered the significance of Jean Vilar's dramatic aesthetic to be diminished by the fact that this great director produced plays at the *Palais de Chaillot*, which is also subsidised, and took his bow before an audience which on first nights included government ministers. No-one says that Roger Planchon and the author he is producing at the *Odéon* are conformists whose creations will consequently be of little value. One law for the rich and one for the poor. Perhaps I am not bringing the same message (for, of course, I am always being reproached or praised for bringing one) but, as we have seen, the critics themselves (those who say that I am bringing a message, for there are others who claim I have not brought any ideological message), do not know what particular ideological message it is.

It is not for me to say: it is up to the critics to find out for themselves; it is their job to be perspicacious.

The 'popular' audience of former times used to wait at the end of the show for the actor who had played the part of the villian in order to lynch him. To-day it is the author whom the critics crudely identify with his characters.

Also, what the author thinks of his work is often confused with the work itself. An English critic concluded that Arthur

Miller was a great author because what Miller said about his own work was interesting: yet the question of his artistic success was not even raised as though it were of quite secondary importance whether Miller had written plays or not, still less whether they were good or bad.

A teacher, in his turn, gently admonishes me for making out a case, at least in principle, for a terroristic nihilism that I defend with a vigour worthy of a better cause. Yet he says my plays would have less force, if they were negative. What does he hold against me then?

Man is alone and in anguish only at certain periods, our own for example, where, goes on the teacher, there is a cleavage that splits society into at least two groups. But does not the character of Hamlet express solitude and anguish? And is not Richard II's cell the prison-house of all our solitudes? It seems to me that solitude and anguish especially characterise the fundamental condition of man. This teacher, who believes that an economic and political revolution will automatically resolve all man's problems, is a utopian. My parrot is more intelligent.

This critic blames me again for wanting to escape from a social framework, for, he says, 'every man is part of a certain civilisation that nurtures him but, he adds, does not totally explain him.'

My plays were never meant to express anything else: just that man is not simply a social animal, a prisoner of his time, but also and above all, at all times, different in his historical context, identical in his essence. So if we can converse with Shakespeare, Molière and Sophocles, if we understand them, it is because they are in their essence profoundly like ourselves. I find that the humanity of universal man is not general and abstract, but real and concrete; and man 'in general' is more

real than man limited to his own period, diminished. Several
times I have said that it is in our fundamental solitude that we
rediscover ourselves and that the more I am alone, the more I
am in communion with others; whereas in organised society,
which is an organisation of functions, man is merely reduced
to his function, which alienates him from the rest.

I would add that it is its fictional power that gives a work
of art its value, for it is above all fictional, a construction of
the imagination; of course one first comes to grips with everything in it that is topical, moral, ideological etc. . . . but this
is grasping the least essential part of it. Is this imaginative
structure, built of course with materials drawn from reality,
of no real use? There are some who think so. But why should
literary construction be less acceptable than pictorial or musical
form? Because it is not so easy to use the latter for propaganda
purposes: as soon as one makes propaganda of them, on the
one hand they change their nature, and on the other they are
too obviously revealed as propaganda. In literature, ambiguity
is easier.

And if some people do not like constructions of the imagination this does not alter the fact that they exist; they are created
because they answer a profound spiritual need.

If there is so much confusion in the appreciation of a work
of art, of a play, it is briefly because no-one knows exactly
what a play or a piece of literature really is. Reread Jean Paulhan's 'Short Preface to all Criticism': he will tell you, infinitely
better than I can, all the different ways of not knowing.

To sum up then, what have I found particularly annoying
in the judgements passed by others? I think what irritated me
above all and what continues to irritate me is that I have not
been judged on the right issue. I feel I have been judged not by

literary critics or by dramatic critics but by moralists. And by moralists I mean fanatical, dogmatic and ideological theologians of every creed. In other words, they beg the question. I am absolutely convinced that it is not this kind of emotional judgement that will finally count. I have also noticed that it is at the time extremely irritating. The subjective moralising of our contemporaries, caught in a storm of passions of every kind, seems to me not only irritating but also blind and blinding. As for the subjective reactions of posterity, these may prove to be just as inacceptable, so that one really does not know where to look for a solution. However, I hope a time for relatively absolute objectivity, if I may so express myself, will one day come when all the storms have passed.

I am going to try and clarify one or two points.   When I declare, for example, that a work of art, a play in this context, should not be ideological, I certainly do not mean one ought not to find ideas or opinions in it. I simply believe it is not the opinions expressed in it that matter.   What matters is the flesh and blood of these ideas, their incarnation, their passion and their life.

A work of art cannot have the same function as an ideology, for if it did it would *be* an ideology, it would no longer be a work of art, that is to say an autonomous creation, an independent universe with its own life and its own laws. I mean that a play, for example, finds its own way, explores itself and must use its own methods to make discovery of certain realities, certain fundamental evidence that reveals itself in the process of creative thinking—for this is what writing is— evidence of an intimate nature (which does not prevent it from joining with the intimate evidence of others, so that in this way solitude ends or may end by identifying itself with the community), intimate evidence that is unexpected at the start and surprising for the author himself, often above all for the author himself. Perhaps this means that imagination is revelation, that it is charged with multiple meanings which a narrow and everyday 'realism' or a limiting ideology can no longer reveal: indeed, when a work of art is compelled simply to illustrate ideology, it is no longer a creative process, action and surprise; it is known in advance. Realist or ideological works can do no more than confirm us in or nail us down to previous and too firmly established positions. Too often what is sought in works of literature is defence and illustration, a demonstration of what has already been and so need not again be demonstrated. This cramps the horizon, it is prison or desert, no more unexpected events, and so no more theatre. It therefore leads me to suggest that realism, for example, is false or unreal and that only the imaginary is true. So a living work of art is one that first of all surprises its own author, escapes from him and throws author and public into disarray, putting them in some way at variance with each other. Otherwise creative work would be pointless, for why give a message that has already been given? A work of art is for me an expression of native intuition that owes almost nothing to other people: by creating a world, by inventing it, the creator discovers it for himself.

A dramatist who has too much control over what he is doing, or a poet whose creative work is intended to be a simple demonstration of this or that, ends by writing something self-sufficient, sealed off from greater potentialities. He is no longer a poet, he is a schoolmaster. I profoundly mistrust drama that is called didactic, for didacticism kills art . . . and instruction too: it is no good always hammering away at the same lesson!

Ideologists more Stalinist than Stalin himself, and some even eminent playwrights, want to save or educate the world at any price. But we know only too well that when religions speak of the salvation of the soul, what they have in mind above all is the hell surely awaiting souls that rebel against salvation; we also know that when education is mentioned one soon ends up with re-education, and we all know what *that* means! It is pedants of every kind, educators and re-educators, propagandists for all kinds of beliefs, theologians and politicians who finally constitute the oppressive forces against which an artist must struggle. I have thought it my duty on several occasions to insist on the two dangers threatening the life of the mind and of the theatre in particular: the mental sluggishness of the bourgeois on the one hand, and on the other the tyranny of political regimes and movements, in other words opposing manifestations of the bourgeois spirit. And by the bourgeois spirit I mean: conformism from above, from below, from the left and the right, bourgeois as well as socialist unreality, dried-up conventional systems. Unfortunately the worst bourgeois are often the anti-bourgeois bourgeois. And I wonder if art might not achieve that liberation, that reapprenticeship to a free mind to which we are no longer accustomed, which we have forgotten, but whose loss is felt as much by those who believe themselves to be free without being so (being prevented by prejudice) as by those who believe they are not or cannot be free.

And yet I believe I am right in thinking that the avant-garde would be the very theatre to contribute to this rediscovery of freedom. I should like to say at once that artistic freedom does not by any means indicate ignorance of laws and standards. Freedom of imagination is not flight into the unreal, it is not escape, it is daring and invention. And invention is not evasion or abdication. The paths of imagination are without number and the inventive powers are boundless. On the contrary, the way is barred only when we find ourselves within the narrow confines of what we call 'some dreary thesis' or realism, whether it be socialist or not. The latter has already withered, its revelations have faded, it is academic and conventional, it is a prison.

(Lecture given at the Sorbonne in March 1960 under the auspices of the '*Maison des lettres*'.)

MY CRITICS AND I

One fine day, some years ago now, I had the idea of making dialogue by stringing together the most commonplace phrases consisting of the most meaningless words and the most worn-out clichés I could find in my own and my friends' vocabulary — and to a lesser extent in foreign conversation manuals.

My initiative was ill-rewarded: overcome by a proliferation of corpse-like words, stunned by the automatism of conversation, I almost gave way to disgust, unspeakable misery, nervous depression and positive asphyxiation. I was, however, able to bring my thankless self-imposed task to its proper conclusion. Quite by chance this text fell into the hands of a young producer who took it for a piece of dramatic writing and turned it into a show. We gave it a title: *La Cantatrice chauve*, and the play caused a great deal of laughter. I was utterly amazed, for I thought I had written the 'Tragedy of language'!

To avoid all possible confusion, I wrote a second play in which one could see how a horrible, sadistic professor went about killing all his unfortunate pupils one by one. The public took this to be highly amusing.

Then, believing I had seen the error of my ways and thinking I was an unconsciously comic author, I wrote some farces: one, among others, was about two almost centenarian characters, amusingly gaga, who organise an evening to which a large number of people are invited, but fail to turn up, for whom an enormous number of unnecessary chairs are collected. A classical situation in vaudeville: the audience knows there is no-one there, the heroes of the play do not; they take the empty chairs for creatures of flesh and blood to whom, pathetically comic, they open their hearts. The audience found this peculiarly macabre.

So once again I had made a mistake. In spite of this I thought I could find a solution that would avoid all possible misunderstanding: I would write not a comedy, or a drama, or a tragedy, but simply a lyrical text, something 'lived'. I transferred to the stage my doubts and my deepest despairs and turned them into dialogue; gave flesh and blood to my inner conflicts, wrote with the greatest sincerity and tore at my entrails: I entitled this *Victimes du devoir*. I was accused of being a humbug, a practical joker.

All right, I said, licking my wounds, why not be a joker?

I set to work and composed seven little sketches, which were performed in one of those theatres on the Left Bank that are called by the strange name of '*avant-garde*'.

This time the critics said I had made a serious attempt at abstract drama and had posed some subtle problems; and yet, however interesting this might be, it could not lead anywhere. I was made to understand that the theatre is not abstract but concrete. I found that this objection — although a little beside the point — was valid.

Then I wanted to make quite sure whether I should persevere or not; and if so, in what direction. Whom should I consult? My critics, obviously. They were the only people who could enlighten me. So I reread and studied with the greatest attention and the greatest respect what these critics had been kind enough to write about my plays. And so I learnt that I had talent: this time, next time, some time, never; that I had humour; that I was completely humourless; that I was a master of the strange and had the temperament of a mystic; that my plays had metaphysical implications; that — according to another—I was basically a realistic spirit, a psychologist, a good observer of the human heart, and that it was in this direction that I should lead my creative work; that I was rather vague; that I wrote clearly and precisely; that my gift of language was poor; that it was rich; that I was a violent critic of contemporary society; that the mysterious flaw in my drama consisted in my failure to denounce an unjust order of society, the established disorder; I was firmly blamed for being a-social; I learnt too that I was in no way poetic and that I ought to be, for 'there is no theatre without poetry'; that I *was* poetic, and that this was just what I should not be, for 'what after all does poetry mean?'; that my drama was too self-conscious, too cold and cerebral; or on the contrary primitive, simple, elementary; that I was entirely lacking in imagination, dry and synoptic; that I had no idea how to organise my excessive and undisciplined imagination and that — instead of being dry and economical as I should be — I was verbose; that, and this was an interesting point in my favour, I would be one of the creators of the drama of objects; 'there should be no props in the theatre', preached another, 'they are no good, what counts is the text'; why yes, props, yes, they are very important, they make the theme of the play more visual, more theatrical; oh no they don't; oh yes they do; oh no . . .

I clasped my head in my hands. I told myself it was better to listen to one critic only. Choosing one at random, I read each of his reviews as they appeared: he blamed my drama for being too facile, for having no secrets; two months later, the same critic objected to an overloading of heavy and obscure symbols and defied anyone to understand what I was about.

'Let's look at another', I said to myself. This second critic pleasantly tickled my pride: I learnt that I had broken all the old theatrical conventions, that I was writing plays that were entirely new, bold and original, that I was an innovator, a revolutionary. Unfortunately this second critic then went back on these ideas and declared I was only carrying on an out-of-date tradition and repeating all that had been said again and again a thousand times before. It was proved to me that I was very much influenced by Strindberg. This forced me to read that Scandinavian dramatist: and I realised it was in fact true. No, not by Strindberg, others affirmed, but rather by Jarry, and that this was good, because I too had a personal offering to make; and that this was not good, as I had no personal offering to make; and by Chekov, Molière, Flaubert, Monnier, Vitrac, Queneau, Picasso, Raymond Roussel, Pirandello, Courteline, Alphonse Allais, Kafka, Lewis Carroll, the Elizabethans, the expressionists, the alienationists with something of Synge and Artaud, not to mention Lautréamont, Rimbaud, Daumier, Napoleon, Richelieu, Mazarin and something of lots of others . . .

Will I be believed when I say I am completely at a loss? I intend to reread one of La Fontaine's old fables: 'The Miller, his Son and the Ass'. Perhaps from that I shall find some satisfactory conclusion.

But unfortunately, it is still someone else's . . .

(*Arts*, 22nd–28th February 1956.)

THE LONDON CONTROVERSY

I

Kenneth Tynan, whose essay 'Theatre and Life' has appeared in France in 'Les jeunes gens en colère vous parlent', is one of the critics who has battled the hardest to make Ionesco known in England. When the battle was won, he suddenly had doubts, which he revealed in 'The Observer' on the 22nd of June, 1958, bearing the interrogative title:

IONESCO: MAN OF DESTINY?

At the Royal Court Theatre, 'The Chairs' is a Court revival, and the Arts Theatre taught us our lesson in 1955. The point of the programme is to demonstrate the versatility of Joan Plowright, who sheds seventy years during the interval; and to celebrate this nimble girl's return from Broadway, where she appeared in both plays under Tony Richardson's direction. Yet there was more in the applause than a mere welcome home. It had about it a blind, deafening intensity: one felt present at the consecration of a cult. Not, let me add, a Plowright cult: staggeringly though she played the crumbling hag in the first play, she simpered a little too knowingly as the crammer's prey in the second. No: this was an Ionesco cult, and in it I smell danger.

Ever since the Fry-Eliot 'poetic revival' caved in on them, the ostriches of our theatrical intelligentsia have been seeking another faith. Anything would do as long as it shook off what are known as 'the fetters of realism.' Now the broad definition of a realistic play is that its characters and events have traceable roots in life; Gorki and Chekhov, Arthur Miller and Tennessee

Williams, Brecht and O'Casey, Osborne and Sartre have all written such plays. They express one man's view of the world in terms of people we can all recognise. Like all hard disciplines, realism can easily be corrupted. It can sink into sentimentality (N. C. Hunter), half-truth (Terence Rattigan), or mere photographic reproduction of the trivia of human behaviour. Even so, those who have mastered it have created the lasting body of twentieth-century drama: and I have been careful not to except Brecht, who employed stylised production techniques to set off essentially realistic characters.

That, for the ostriches, was what ruled him out of court. He was too real. Similarly, they preferred Beckett's '*Fin de Partie*', in which the human element was minimal, to 'Waiting for Godot,' which not only contained two tramps of mephitic reality but even seemed to regard them, as human beings, with love. Veiling their disapproval, the ostriches seized on Beckett's more blatant verbal caprices and called them 'authentic images of a disintegrated society.' But it was only when M. Ionesco arrived that they hailed a messiah. Here at last was a self-proclaimed advocate of *anti-théâtre:* explicitly anti-realist, and by implication anti-reality as well. Here was a writer ready to declare that words were meaningless and that all communication between human beings was impossible. The aged (as in 'The Chairs') are wrapped in an impenetrable cocoon of hallucinatory memories; they can speak intelligibly neither to each other nor to the world. The teacher in 'The Lesson' can 'get through' to his pupil only by means of sexual assault, followed by murder. Words, the magic innovation of our species, are dismissed as useless and fraudulent.

Ionesco's is a world of isolated robots, conversing in cartoon-strip balloons of dialogue that are sometimes hilarious, sometimes evocative, and quite often neither, on which occasions they become profoundly tiresome. (As with shaggy-dog stories, few of M. Ionesco's plays survive a second hearing: I felt this particularly with 'The Chairs.') This world is not mine, but I recognise it to be a valid personal vision, presented with great imaginative aplomb and verbal audacity. The peril arises when it is held up for general emulation as the gateway to the theatre of the future, that bleak new world from which the humanist heresies of faith in logic and belief in man will forever be banished.

M. Ionesco certainly offers an 'escape from realism': but an escape into what? A blind alley, perhaps, adorned with *tachiste* murals. Or a self-imposed vacuum, wherein the author ominously bids us observe the absence of air. Or, best of all, a funfair ride on a ghost train, all skulls and hooting waxworks, from which we emerge into the far more intimidating clamour of diurnal reality. M. Ionesco's theatre is pungent and exciting, but it remains a diversion. It is not on the main road: and we do him no good, nor the drama at large, to pretend that it is . . .

II

Ionesco replies to Kenneth Tynan as follows:

THE PLAYWRIGHT'S ROLE

I was of course honoured by the article Mr Tynan devoted to my two plays, 'The Chairs' and 'The Lesson', in spite of the strictures it contained, which a critic has a perfect right to make. However, since some of his objections seem to me to be based on premises that are not only false but, strictly speaking, outside the domain of the theatre, I think I have the right to make certain comments.

In effect, Mr Tynan says that it has been claimed, and that I myself have approved or supported this claim, that I was a sort of 'messiah' of the theatre. This is doubly untrue because I do not like messiahs and I certainly do not consider the vocation of the artist or the playwright to lie in that direction. I have a distinct impression that it is Mr Tynan who is in search of messiahs. But to deliver a message to the world, to wish to direct its course, to save it, is the business of the founders of religions, of the moralists or the politicians — who, incidentally, as we know only too well, make a pretty poor job of it. A playwright simply writes plays, in which he can offer only a testimony, not a didactic message — a personal, affective testimony of his anguish and the anguish of others or, which is rare, of his happiness — or he can express his feelings, comic or tragic, about life.

A work of art has nothing to do with doctrine. I have already written elsewhere that any work of art which was ideological and nothing else would be pointless, tautological, inferior to the doctrine it claimed to illustrate, which would already have been expressed in its proper language, that of discursive demonstration. An ideological play can be no more than the vulgarisation of an ideology. In my view, a work of art has its own unique system of expression, its own means of directly apprehending the real.

Mr Tynan seems to accuse me of being deliberately, explicitly, anti-realist; of having declared that words have no meaning and that all language is incommunicable. That is only partly true, for the very fact of writing and presenting plays is surely incompatible with such a view. I simply hold that it is difficult to make oneself understood, not absolutely impossible, and my play 'The Chairs' is a plea, pathetic perhaps, for mutual understanding. As for the idea of reality, Mr Tynan seems (as he also made clear in an interview published in *Encounter*) to acknowledge only one plane of reality: what is called the 'social' plane, which seems to me to be the most external, in other words the most superficial. That is why I think that writers like Sartre (Sartre the author of political melodramas), Osborne, Miller, Brecht, etc, are simply the new *auteurs du boulevard*, representatives of a left-wing conformism which is just as lamentable as the right-wing sort. These writers offer nothing that one does not know already, through books and political speeches.

But that is not all; it is not enough to be a social realist writer, one must also, apparently, be a militant believer in what is known as progress. The only worth-while authors, those who are on the 'main road' of the theatre, would be those who thought in a certain clearly defined way, obeying certain pre-established principles or directives. This would be to make the 'main road' a very narrow one; it would considerably restrict the planes of reality (which are innumerable) and limit the field open to the investigations of artistic research and creation.

I believe that what separates us all from one another is simply society itself, or, if you like, politics. This is what raises barriers between men, this is what creates misunderstanding.

If I may be allowed to express myself paradoxically, I should say that the true society, the authentic human community, is extra-social — a wider, deeper society, that which is revealed by our common anxieties, our desires, our secret nostalgias. The whole history of the world has been governed by these nostalgias and anxieties, which political action does no more than reflect and interpret, very imperfectly. No society has been able to abolish human sadness, no political system can deliver us from the pain of living, from our fear of death, our thirst for the absolute; it is the human condition that directs the social condition, not vice versa.

This 'reality' seems to me much vaster and more complex than the one to which Mr Tynan and many others want to limit themselves. The problem is to get to the source of our malady, to find the non-conventional language of this anguish, perhaps by breaking down this 'social' language which is nothing but clichés, empty formulas, and slogans. The 'robot' characters Mr Tynan disapproves of seem to me to be precisely those who belong *solely* to this or that *milieu* or social 'reality', who are prisoners of it, and who — being no more than social, seeking a solution to their problems only by so-called social means — have become impoverished, alienated, empty. It is precisely the conformist, the *petit-bourgeois*, the ideologist of *every* society who is lost and dehumanised. If anything needs demystifying it is our ideologies, which offer ready-made solutions (which history quickly overtakes and refutes) and a language that congeals *as soon as it is formulated*. It is these ideologies which must be continually re-examined in the light of our anxieties and dreams, and their congealed language must be relentlessly split apart in order to find the living sap beneath.

To discover the fundamental problem common to all mankind, I must ask myself what *my* fundamental problem is, what *my* most ineradicable fear is. I am certain, then, to find the problems and fears of literally everyone. That is the true road, into my own darkness, our darkness, which I try to bring to the light of day.

D

It would be amusing to try an experiment, which I have no room for here but which I hope to carry out some day. I could take almost any work of art, any play, and guarantee to give it in turn a Marxist, a Buddhist, a Christian, an Existentialist, a psycho-analytical interpretation and 'prove' that the work subjected to each interpretation is a perfect and exclusive illustration of each creed, that it confirms this or that ideology beyond all doubt. For me this proves another thing: that every work of art (unless it is a pseudo-intellectualist work, a work already comprised in some ideology that it merely illustrates, as with Brecht) is outside ideology, is not reducible to ideology. Ideology circumscribes without penetrating it. The absence of ideology in a work does not mean an absence of ideas: on the contrary it fertilises them. In other words, it was not Sophocles who was inspired by Freud but, obviously, the other way round. Ideology is not the source of art. A work of art is the source and the raw material of ideologies to come.

What, then, should the critic do? Where should he look for his criteria? Inside the work itself, its universe and its mythology. He must look at it, listen to it, and simply say whether it is true to its own nature. The best judgment is a careful exposition of the work itself. For that, the work must be allowed to speak, uncoloured by preconception or prejudice.

Whether or not it is on the 'main road'; whether or not it is what you would like it to be — to consider this is already to pass judgment, a judgment that is external, pointless and false. A work of art is the expression of an incommunicable reality that one tries to communicate — and which sometimes can be communicated. That is its paradox, and its truth.

(Eugène IONESCO).

III

Ionesco's reply provoked numerous comments. Kenneth Tynan replied to this reply. Then Philip Toynbee had his say, as well as a number of readers whose letters were published. Two fragments from these letters are given.

But here, first of all, is Kenneth Tynan again. This article appeared in 'The Observer' on the 6th of July, 1958:

IONESCO AND THE PHANTOM

M. Ionesco's article on 'The Playwright's Role' is discussed elsewhere in these pages by Mr Toynbee and several readers. I want to add what I hope will not be a postscript, for this is a debate that should continue.

As I read the piece I felt first bewilderment, next admiration, and finally regret. Bewilderment at his assumption that I wanted drama to be forced to echo a particular political creed, when all I want is for drama to realise that it is a *part* of politics, in the sense that every human activity, even buying a packet of cigarettes, has social and political repercussions. Then, admiration: no one could help admiring the sincerity and skill with which, last Sunday, M. Ionesco marshalled prose for his purposes. And ultimately, regret: regret that a man so capable of stating a positive attitude towards art should deny that there was any positive attitude worth taking towards life. Or even (which is crucial) that there was an umbilical connection between the two.

The position towards which M. Ionesco is moving is that which regards art as if it were something different from and independent of everything else in the world; as if it not only did not but *should* not correspond to anything outside the mind of the artist. This position, as it happens, was reached some years ago by a French painter who declared that, since nothing in nature exactly resembled anything else, he proposed to burn all of his paintings which in any way resembled anything that already existed. The end of that line, of course, is Action Painting.

M. Ionesco has not yet gone so far. He is stuck, to pursue the analogy, in an earlier groove, the groove of cubism, which has fascinated him so much that he has begun to confuse ends and means. The cubists employed distortion to make discoveries about the nature of objective reality. M. Ionesco, I fear, is on the brink of believing that his distortions are more valid and important than the external world it is their proper function to interpret. To adapt Johnson, I am not yet so lost in drama criticism as to forget that plays are the daughters of earth, and that things are the sons of heaven. But M. Ionesco is in danger of forgetting; of locking himself up in that hall of mirrors which in philosophy is known as solipsism.

Art is parasitic on life, just as criticism is parasitic on art. M. Ionesco and his followers are breaking the chain, applying the tourniquet, aspiring as writers to a condition of stasis. At their best, of course, they don't succeed: the alarming thing is that they try. As in physiology, note how quickly the brain, starved of blood, produces hallucinations and delusions of grandeur. 'A work of art,' says M. Ionesco, 'is the source and the raw material of ideologies to come.' O hubris! Art and ideology often interact on each other; but the plain fact is that both spring from a common source. Both draw on human experience to explain mankind to itself; both attempt, in very different ways, to assemble coherence from seemingly unrelated phenomena; both stand guard for us against chaos. They are brothers, not child and parent. To say, as M. Ionesco does, that Freud was inspired by Sophocles is the direst nonsense. Freud merely found in Sophocles confirmation of a theory he had formed on a basis of empirical evidence. This does not make Sophocles a Freudian, or vice versa: it is simply a pleasing instance of fraternal corroboration.

You may wonder why M. Ionesco is so keen on this phantom notion of art as a world of its own, answerable to none but its own laws. Wonder no more: he is merely seeking to exempt himself from any kind of value-judgment. His aim is to blind us to the fact that we are all in some sense critics, who bring to the theatre not only those 'nostalgias and anxieties' by which, as he rightly says, world history has largely been governed, but also a whole series of new ideas — moral, social, psychological, political — through which we hope some day to free ourselves from the rusty hegemony of *Angst*. These fond ideas, M. Ionesco quickly assures us, do not belong in the theatre. Our job, as critics, is just to hear the play and 'simply say whether it is true to its own nature'. Not, you notice, whether it is true to ours; or even relevant; for we, as an audience, have forfeited our right to a hearing as conscious, sentient beings. 'Clear evidence of cancer here, sir.' 'Very well, leave it alone: it's being true to its own nature.'

Whether M. Ionesco admits it or not, every play worth serious consideration is a statement. It is a statement addressed in the first person singular to the first person plural; and the latter must retain the right of dissent. I am rebuked in the current *Encounter* for having disagreed with the nihilistic philosophy expressed in Strindberg's 'Dream Play': 'The important thing,' says my interviewer, 'seems to me to be not the rightness of Strindberg's belief, but rather how he has expressed it . . .' Strindberg expressed it very vividly, but there are things more important than that. If a man tells me something I believe to be an untruth, am I forbidden to do more than congratulate him on the brilliance of his lying?

Cyril Connolly once said, once and wanly, that it was closing time in the gardens of the West; but I deny the rest of that suavely cadenced sentence, which asserts that 'from now on an artist will be judged only by the resonance of his solitude or the quality of his despair.' Not by me, he won't. I shall, I hope, respond to the honesty of such testimonies: but I shall be looking for something more, something harder; for evidence of the artist who is not content with the passive role of a symptom, but concerns himself, from time to time, with such things as healing. M. Ionesco correctly says that no ideology has yet abolished fear, pain or sadness. Nor has any work of art. But both are in the business of trying. What other business is there?

(Kenneth TYNAN)

IV

Philip Toynbee expressed his opinion in a review of Arthur Miller's plays on July the 6th, 1958:

AN ATTITUDE TO LIFE (EXTRACTS)

In last week's 'Observer' M. Eugène Ionesco wrote as follows: ' . . . writers like Sartre, Osborne, Miller, Brecht, etc, are simply the new *auteurs du boulevard*, representatives of a left-wing conformism which is just as lamentable as the right-wing sort. These writers offer nothing that one does not know already, through books and political speeches.' He went on to write: 'I believe that what separates us all from one another is simply society itself, or if you like, politics. This is what raises barriers between men, this is what creates misunderstanding.'

The first of these quotations strongly suggests that Sartre is the only playwright M. Ionesco has read or seen of those whom he has chosen to attack. It certainly seems unlikely that M. Ionesco is well acquainted with the work of Arthur Miller, for the charge against him of 'left-wing conformism' is as absurd as it would be to charge M. Ionesco with being the mouth-piece of the Algerian *colons*.

As for the second quotation from M. Ionesco's article, it seems to me to underline, by its frivolity, one of the very qualities which make Arthur Miller an important playwright and Eugène Ionesco a lesser one. To write that what separates us all from one another is simply 'society itself' ('*le social*') is like writing that the human race is horribly hampered in its freedom of movement by the atmosphere which lies so heavy on our planet.

(Philip TOYNBEE)

V

And here are the opinions of two 'Observer' readers. The second letter ends with a phrase that could have been from the pen of Robert Kemp:

Sir,

M. Ionesco has a view of life, a view of history and even a view of the future. These constitute an ideology just as definite as Kenneth Tynan's.

M. Ionesco's article of faith is that 'no political system can deliver us from the pain of living, from our fear of death, our thirst for the absolute.' He also believes that everything outside himself is 'superficial'.

The majority of mankind look to political systems for

something different: to deliver them from poverty and unnecessary death and to satisfy their thirst for knowledge. They have also discovered that their relationships with other men involve life and death.

(John BERGER
Newland, Glos.)

Sir,

I am anything but an addict of Eugène Ionesco's plays: what I know of them seems to me distasteful and — to use his own term — incommunicable. But I consider his reply to Mr Tynan's criticism one of the most brilliant refutations of the current theory of 'social realism'. This essay should be reprinted and distributed on the widest possible scale. If only M. Ionesco were able to put some of its clarity and wisdom into his own plays — he might yet become a great playwright!

(H. F. GARTEN
London, s.w.10)

VI

Then an imposing personality intervened in the debate: Orson Welles. He gave his opinion on what the playwright's role should be in an article published by 'The Observer' on the 13th of July:

THE ARTIST AND THE CRITIC

M. Eugène Ionesco's recent article in reply to Kenneth Tynan offers, it seems to me, some inadvertent testimony in support of the playwright's celebrated views on the general unreliability of language.

M. Ionesco seems to imagine that 'The Observer's critic has

ordered him, like a sort of traffic policeman, on to 'the main road'. In fact, the remarks to which he takes exception were not addressed to the artist or his art; what was deplored was the peculiar ardour of his audience. As one of Mr Ionesco's enthusiasts, I felt that Mr Tynan rather overstated his case. A keen admirer is not the follower of a cult; and I did not like being told that to enjoy a play is necessarily to approve its 'message'. When I applauded 'The Chairs' was I participating in a demonstration in favour of nihilism? This sounded far-fetched. After reading M. Ionesco's rebuttal to Mr Tynan I am not so sure.

If man cannot communicate, can he be expected to control his destiny? Mr Tynan's gloomiest deductions would seem to be justified if M. Ionesco admits the ultimate logic of his proposition: that proving the incapacity of language, he also proves the incapacity of man himself.

Can the artist evade politics? He should certainly avoid polemics. Directing the course of the world, writes M. Ionesco, 'is the business of the founders of religions, of the moralists or the politicians.' An artist's every word is an expression of a social attitude; and I cannot agree with M. Ionesco that these expressions are always less original than political speeches or pamphlets. An artist must confirm the values of his society; or he must challenge them.

Giving, as he does, such emphasis to the wholly personal in art, to the individual, the unique, M. Ionesco surely knows better than to look for sanctuary among the authoritarians. He cannot hope to smuggle his own private world into a world where privacy is a crime, where the sovereign individual is an outlaw. He throws himself — frigidly aloof, proudly inviolable — on the mercy of the partisans of freedom.

I resist the delicate instinct which tempts me to apologise to M. Ionesco for the use of that word 'freedom'. Whatever is valuable is likely to have a rather shopsoiled name. Very few of us, however, are so fed up with talk about freedom that we are ready to scuttle freedom of speech. In M. Ionesco's country that freedom cannot be said to be any safer than elsewhere just at this moment. Many freedoms everywhere are under siege, and all of them — including M. Ionesco's privilege to shrug his shoulders at politics — were, at one time or another, political achievements. It is not 'politics' which is the arch-enemy of art; it is neutrality — which robs us of the sense of tragedy. Neutrality is also a political position like any other; and its practical consequences have been meditated by many of M. Ionesco's fellow poets in the only effective ivory tower to be erected in our century — the concentration camp.

That politics is best left to the professionals is a perfectly respectable conservative argument; but M. Ionesco was careful to add that in his view the politicians 'make a pretty poor job of it'. I wish it could be said that these two sentiments — the revolutionary and the legitimist — cancel each other out. But M. Ionesco, for once, is not talking Jabberwocky: he is talking surrender.

To denounce leadership as incompetent, and, having done so, then to insist that the 'direction' of world affairs be left strictly in these incompetent hands, is to acknowledge an extraordinary despair.

Under the present circumstances, the call to abandon ship is not merely unpractical: it is a cry of panic. If we are doomed indeed, let M. Ionesco go down fighting with the rest of us. He should have the courage of our platitudes.

(Orson WELLES)

VII

The debate could go on for ever. To finish it off (provisionally) we give the text of Ionesco's second reply to Kenneth Tynan. This text is unpublished. 'The Observer' bought the English rights but did not publish it.

HEARTS ARE NOT WORN ON THE SLEEVE

I cannot answer all the problems raised by my courteous enemy, Mr Kenneth Tynan, in his last article (*Ionesco and the Phantom*). It would take too long and I cannot go on abusing the hospitality of 'The Observer'. It would also, in a way, be a waste of time, for we would only succeed in repeating ourselves. That is what Mr Kenneth Tynan is already beginning to do. So I shall try above all to put my views in greater detail and answer those questions which seem to me essential.

Mr Tynan reproaches me for being so fascinated by the means of expressing 'objective reality' (but it is another question to know what objective reality really is), — that I forget objective reality in favour of the means of expressing it, which therefore becomes an end in itself. In other words, he is, I believe, accusing me of formalism. But what is the history of art or literature if it is not, first and foremost, the history of its expression, the history of its language or idiom? For me expression is form and content at one and the same time. To approach the problem of literature by studying its expression (and that, in my opinion, is what a critic should do) is also to deal with its content and arrive at its essence. But to attack an idiom that is out of date, to try and hold it up to ridicule and reveal its limitations and its deficiencies; to try and shake it up, for every idiom wears out, gets hidebound and is drained of significance; to try and renew it or reinvent it or simply to amplify it is the function of every 'creator', who in so doing, as

I have just said, reaches the heart of things, of living and changing reality, always different and yet always the same. This process can take place consciously as well as instinctively, with humour, if you like, and in perfect freedom, with ideas but without ideology, if ideology means a closed system of thought a system of slogans, good, bad or indifferent, far removed from life, which it quite fails to absorb, although it persists in trying to impose itself as though it were the expression of life itself. I am not the first to point out the divergency that exists, in art as well as in 'political' life, between ideology and reality. I therefore consider art to be more concerned with an independent search for knowledge than with any system of morals, political or not. It is of course a way of knowing that involves the emotions, an exploration that is objective in its subjectivity, testimony rather than teaching, evidence of how the world appears to the artist.

To renew one's idiom or one's language is to renew one's conception or one's vision of the world. A revolution is a change of mentality. Any new artistic expression enriches us by answering some spiritual need and broadens the frontiers of known reality; it is an adventure, it is a gamble, so it cannot be a repetition of some already classified ideology, it cannot serve any other kind of truth but its own (because a truth, once uttered, is already superseded). Any work that answers this requirement may seem strange at the outset, since it communicates what has not been communicated before in this particular way. And as everything is to be found in its expression, its structure or inner logic, it is the expression that must be examined. In a reasoned argument one should see that the conclusion follows logically from the data; for it is a construction that seems (but only *seems*) to be independent, to stand alone —

just as a play, for example, is a construction one has to describe in order to verify its internal unity. The data used in any reasoning process are of course verified by other reasoned arguments, which are also again constructions.

I do not believe there is any contradiction between creation and knowledge, for mental structures are probably a reflection of the structure of the universe.

What is the point of a temple, a church or a palace? Can we find any realism there? Certainly not. Yet architecture reveals the fundamental laws of construction; every building testifies to the *objective* reality of the principles of architecture. And what is the purpose of a building? Of a church? Apparently to accommodate people and shelter the faithful. But that is their least important use. Their principal purpose is to reveal and be the expression of these architectonic laws, and it is in order to study and admire these buildings that we visit abandoned temples, cathedrals, deserted palaces and old, uninhabitable houses. Is it then the purpose of all these buildings to improve the lot of man (which according to Mr Tynan should be the essential aim of all thought and all works of art)? Certainly not. And what also is the purpose of music, unless it be to reveal its own different laws? In a sense one could therefore say that a column or a sonata is of no practical use at all. Their purpose is to be what they are. The one should just stand there, the other should be heard. And what is the point of the existence of the universe? Simply that it should exist. But whether it is of any use to existence to exist is a matter of opinion and a different question, an unthinkable one moreover, for existence cannot but exist.

When Mr Tynan defends realist writers, because they express themselves in an idiom everyone can immediately recognise, he is nevertheless defending a narrow realism — even if he denies it — the kind of realism that no longer captures reality and must therefore be exploded. Once a thing is admitted by all, it is no longer admissible.

There was, at the beginning of this century, what is usually called a vast '*avant-garde*' in all realms of the spirit. A revolution, an upheaval in our mental habits. Exploration continues, of course, and intelligence perseveres in its research, which in turn transforms intelligence itself and completely alters our understanding of the world. In the West the renewal continues, particularly in music and painting. In literature and especially in the theatre this movement seems to have come to a halt, round about 1925 perhaps. I should like to be allowed the hope that I may be considered one of the modest craftsmen who are trying to take it further. I have attempted, for example, to exteriorise, by using objects, the anguish (I hope Mr Tynan will excuse me employing this word) of my characters, to make the set speak and the action on the stage more visual, to translate into con- concrete images terror, regret or remorse, and estrangement, to play with words (but not to send them packing) and even perhaps to deform them, — which is generally accepted in the work of poets and humorists. I have thus sought to extend the idiom of the theatre. I believe I have to some degree succeeded in my aim. Is this to be condemned? I do not know. All I know is that I have not been judged on the merit of these plays, for this does not seem to be one of the considerations of a dramatic critic as important as Mr Tynan, who is moreover far from blind.

But let us come back to realism for the last time. Quite recently I happened to see an international exhibition of painting. There were 'abstract' pictures (which do not seem to

appeal to Mr Tynan) and representational pictures: impressionist, post-impressionist and 'social-realist'. In the Soviet pavilion,
of course, only the latter were in evidence. These paintings
were dead: portraits of heroes frozen into conventional and unreal poses; sailors and snipers in captured castles, so academic
they were no longer credible; and non-political pictures too, a
few frosty flowers; and a street scene with *abstract* city folk, and
in the centre a woman devoid of life, inexpressive though exact
in detail, dehumanised. It was very curious. And what was even
more curious was that the sturdy local bourgeois were lost in
admiration. They said that this particular pavilion was the only
one worth seeing; for even the Fauves or the Impressionists
went over their heads. This was not the first time I had noticed
that the reactions of Stalinist bourgeois realists and Capitalist
bourgeois realists are identical. By a still more curious trick of
fate, it is clear that these social-realist painters were in fact
formalist and academic, unable to emphasise content just because they neglected the requirements of form. The content had
escaped them and formal technique had turned against them
and taken revenge by extinguishing reality.

In the French pavilion, on the other hand, the pictures by
Masson (a painter who is indeed exclusively concerned with the
way he paints, his means of expression, his technique) gave
evidence of a deeply moving truth, of an extraordinary
pictorially dramatic quality. Dark night surrounds a dazzlingly
brilliant throbbing light and struggles to overcome it. Curves
trace a pattern, lines rear up violently and through a gap in the
serried planes of composition we can glimpse infinite space.
As Masson, the craftsman, had left human reality strictly alone,
as he had not tried to track it down and thought of nothing but
'the act of painting', human reality and the tragedy of it had

for this very reason, truly and freely, been unveiled. So it was what Mr Tynan calls anti-reality that had become real, the incommunicable was communicated; and it is there too, behind an apparent rejection of all concrete and moral human truth, that his living heart was hidden, whereas with the others, the anti-formalists, there was nothing but dried-up forms, dead and empty: hearts are not worn on the sleeve.

Mr Tynan agrees with me when he remarks that 'no ideology has yet abolished fear, pain or sadness. Nor has any work of art. But both are in the business of trying. What other business is there?'

What other business? Painting, for example. Or having a sense of humour. No Englishman should be without that. I beg of you, Mr Tynan, do not attempt, by means of art or any other means, to improve the lot of mankind. Please do not do it. We have had enough of civil wars already, enough of blood and tears and trials that are a mockery, enough of 'righteous' executioners and 'ignoble' martyrs, of disappointed hopes and penal servitude.

Do not improve the lot of mankind, if you really wish them well.

A few words for Mr Philip Toynbee. I take back all the wicked things I said about Arthur Miller. Mr Toynbee judges Mr Arthur Miller's plays according to this dramatist's own ideas about writing drama. I did not think this could be anything but a presumption in his favour. No doubt I was wrong. So I am going to make a favourable judgement of his work too. according to something that lies outside the work itself. I shall therefore judge Mr Arthur Miller's work according to the photograph of Mr Miller published in 'The Observer'. Mr Miller does indeed look a very fine fellow. And so I admire his work.

On the other hand, I am rather amazed that Mr Philip

Toynbee should be amazed at the idea that man can be hampered in his movements by society or by the air he breathes. It
seems to me it is not so easy to breathe and to live; I also think
it possible for man not to be a social animal. A child has great
difficulty in fitting into society, he struggles against it and finds
it hard to adapt himself to it: those who work with children
will know what I am talking about. And if a child finds it hard
to adapt himself to society, it is because there is in human
nature something that has to escape the social order or be
alienated by it. And even when a man becomes part of society,
he does not always manage things very well. Social life, living
with other people and what that can mean, has been shown to
us by Sartre himself (Mr Toynbee will not object to me
quoting Sartre) in his play *Huis-Clos*. Society is hell, hell is
other people. We would be very pleased to do without them.
And was it not Dostoievsky who said that one could not live
more than a few days with anyone before beginning to detest
him? And does not the hero of *Homme pour homme* lose his soul
and his name, and does he not lose his individuality to the
point of becoming totally alienated when he joins in the
collective irresponsibility of the wearers of uniform?

I too have done my military service. My sergeant-major
despised me because my boots were not well polished. How
could I make him understand that there are other standards of
judgement apart from polishing boots? And that shining my
boots did not entirely exhaust my possibilities as a human
being? At dances, girls did not want me as a partner because I
was not a lieutenant. And yet, out of uniform, I was still a man.
As for my general, he was so morally deformed that he thought
of himself as nothing but a general, and used to go to bed in his
uniform. Later on I worked as a clerk, yet I still had the feeling

I was 'something more' than a clerk. I believe I was really well aware of my estrangement from society, the kind of alienation that is denounced by the most Marxist of the Marxists and prevents a man from developing freely and finding fulfilment. When my play, *Les Chaises*, was performed in Warsaw and a few other Polish towns my characters were immediately seen to be not mentally deranged but socially estranged. And yet they wore the working clothes of the proletariat, of 'the workers'. I believe that every society alienates, even and above all a 'socialist' society (in the West, in England or in France, the classes are levelled out or interpenetrate more freely) where the political leaders consider themselves an elite because they are enlightened and where they are absorbed as men by their function. Wherever one finds social functions, one finds alienation (society being an organisation of functions), for once again man is not merely a social function.

When my lieutenant and my boss are back in their homes, alone in their rooms, they could, for example, just like me, being outside the social order, be afraid of death as I am, have the same dreams and nightmares, and having stripped off their social personality, suddenly find themselves naked, like a body stretched out on the sand, amazed to be there and amazed at their own amazement, amazed at their own awareness as they are confronted with the immense ocean of the infinite, alone in the brilliant, inconceivable and indisputable sunlight of exis-tence. And it is then that my general or my boss can be identi-fied with me. It is in our solitude that we can all be reunited. And that is why true society transcends our social machinery.

But that has nothing to do with the theatre. *Je m'excuse*. I am sorry.   (Eugene IONESCO,
republished in *Cahiers des Saisons*, Winter 1959.)

INTERVIEWS

You have said that only reality can turn into a nightmare. What do you mean by that?

From time to time my characters make jokes or express themselves in a humorous way; they also say stupid things; or else they express themselves awkwardly, they do not really understand themselves, in their own clumsy way they are trying to get to know themselves; they are like the majority of men, they don't utter pearls of wisdom every time they open their mouths; they may also contradict what *I* think or what a contrasting character thinks. It was not I who said that 'it was reality, not dreams, that turned into a nightmare': it was one of my characters who made this remark. So you have to know about this character: whether he was serious or making fun, in what situation he said what he said and why, what he meant by it . . . etc . . . And above all is he really able to say what he means? You should ask my characters these questions, not me.

But what part does the individual play in this 'nightmare reality'? Does this mean that we dream reality? Or that the dream is reality?

Now if you are asking my personal opinion about this 'nightmare reality' I admit, just between ourselves, that I really do feel that life is nightmarish, painful and unbearable, like a bad dream. Look around you: wars, catastrophes and disasters, hatred and persecution, confusion, death lying in wait for all of us, we talk without understanding one another, we struggle as best we may in a world that appears to be in the grip of some terrible fever; is not man, as has been said, the sick animal?

Have we not the impression that the real is unreal, that it is not really for us? That this world is not out true world? If it were, why should we want to change things? We would not even know it was imperfect or be aware of evil. But what is even more strange is that we are attached to this nightmare reality and are scandalised not so much by the horror of it as by its precariousness. It is in our nature to understand everything, and we understand very little: we cannot understand ourselves. We are created to live together and we tear one another to pieces; we do not want to die, so we are meant to be immortal, but we *do* die. It is horrible and cannot be taken seriously. How can I trust in a world that has no stability, that flits away? One moment I can see Camus, I can see Atlan, and suddenly they are gone. It's ridiculous. It almost makes me laugh. Anyway, King Solomon has already exhausted this subject.

Is the world just an illusion? I cannot tell you. Apply to the metaphysicians of the East if you want enlightenment about that. In fact, it is of little account: it appears to us as reality and it is obviously with this reality (however precarious it may be) that we have to struggle.

Is there a social reality? And if so, as an artist, do you make use of this reality because its nature is both oneirical and social?

Of course there is such a thing as social, individual, biological, physical reality etc . . . human reality, that is to say reality as it may appear to men. What other reality could there be?

Besides, in one sense, everything is social. I believe, however, that man cannot be explained merely by his social organisation, his social machinery. Also, I have already said, stretching my terms a little, that the deepest level of society is extra-social. Are our essential dreams not the same? Do they not reveal our common anxieties, our common desires? And does not social organisation alienate us all? It is just for this reason that there are 'a-social' people. When I am most profoundly myself, I join a forgotten community. Often society (external) alienates me, that is to say it estranges me both from myself and from other people. I prefer the word 'community' to words like 'social, sociology' etc . . . This extra-historical community seems to me fundamental. We can join it beyond barriers (and barricades), beyond caste and class etc . . . It has often been said that man is a sociable animal. But you have only to see what goes on in the *Métro*: all the passengers make a dive for the single seats. And in buses the seat that is always occupied is the one right at the front of the vehicle, where the passenger can sit alone. Ants, bees and birds are sociable. Man, however, is a-sociable. Yet he is still social, this is inevitable.

Being a-social still means in the long run being social in a different way. Only nowadays, by accident or design, a great number of misunderstandings are concealed in the word 'social'. Thus it is said that any sort of work or activity should have some social interest: this often means it should have some political interest, (i.e. express the tendencies of a particular political movement), be of practical use or serve the purposes of propaganda.

To return to the oneirical aspect of my own work; as you ask me the question, I must tell you that when I dream I do not feel I am abdicating thought. On the contrary, I have the impression that as I dream I see evident truths that appear before me more brilliantly illumined, more ruthlessly penetrating than in my waking state, when everything often seems more mellow, more uniform and impersonal. That is why in my drama I utilize images drawn from my dreams, realities that have been dreamed.

You also say that you do not explain, but that you explain your-self. What is a witness who explains himself?

When I say that I am a witness, what I really mean is that I am not a judge. I do not preside over the court, neither am I the public prosecutor or the counsel for the defence. Whether the witness has been chosen by the defence or the prosecution is of no concern to him. The witness (in theory!) does not declare himself. If he is upright, he should be objective . . . within the limits of his own subjectivity. The prosecutor who assails the defendant (that is his function) and the counsel who protects him (that is his job) are tendentious, partisan: they are dealing in . . . politics and strategy. The magistrate is like the Pope, the Head of the State, and all those who — Bible, Code and Dogma in hand — dare to sit in judgement.

The witness tells a story, or not even that; he expounds how certain facts have appeared to him. He tells the truth . . . a subjective truth, of course.

He does, after all, use a little judgement; he cannot help it. But the perfect witness should not be a judge, because he should not be prejudiced.

I do not explain, no. I am a witness, that is to say subject to the explanations and interpretations of others. But I explain myself. That is to say, when the judges find my exposition not clear enough, I try to clarify it. This is exactly what you are making me do at this moment. I chiefly try to clarify myself when (and this often happens) people want to make me say things I have not said.

So a witness (that is to say: a poet) gives an account of the world as it appears to him. But bearing witness is always a kind of re-creation, or creation, since everything is subjective. We know too how similar subjective reactions can be. Objectivity is therefore a concensus of subjective reactions. So to come back to the question you asked just now, it is not too risky to say that we all dream collectively the same reality, for it is only what we imagine it to be.

In a court of law, it is the witness who is the freest man. And after him the defendant, even if he is in chains. The real prisoners are the judges, prisoners of their code, of their dogma. They do not even have the freedom to react subjectively, as they are subject to juridical standards.

It is annoying to be judged, but not so serious as one thinks: when the case has been heard there are always Courts of Appeal. An indefinite number of Courts of Appeal. If judgment can vary, recorded testimony remains the same. Something paradoxical happens: testimony (which of course testifies *to* something) takes on in the end a kind of validity of its own, becomes permanent and autonomous, whereas courts of law move round the testimony, succeed and contradict one another. Laws and viewpoints change.

You have of course realised that this testimony is the work of art, that these courts of law are societies, historicity.

Courts of law are not serious: they are theatre, a theatrical ceremony.

So your theatre has after all a role to play as a mirror for your public. In what shape or form should people rediscover themselves in your theatre?

Of course it has. I hope so. Considering that I am, I repeat, like everyone else, at my deepest level; while still remaining myself. A-social people should at least be able to recognise themselves.

But the social surface of myself is impersonal. There is very little of myself there.

People have tried to define bourgeois man, proletarian man, man the artisan, the soldier, the husband, etc. . . . . Don't you agree that man the artisan, the soldier etc. . . . . is not all of man? That you dehumanise him by 'sociologising' him? Don't you agree that you alienate him by labelling him in this way? And that you dispossess him precisely of what is essential? And that there is another 'unsociologised' community — the one I mentioned a moment ago?

You have said that your public ought even to feel embarrassed. Doesn't this suggest a didactic element in your plays, although you deny it?

I think I did say that once: in the stage directions written for the actors in *Jacques ou la Soumission*. I wanted something 'painful' in their acting in order to convey to the audience a kind of unease that would correspond to the absurdity of the characters.

You see that as didacticism. Obviously one can learn a lesson from anything, even from a lesson, if one really wants to; and I am sure it is a very good thing to do. So one could say that everything is a lesson. One could also call a chair a table if I were to use it as a table. And in such a case it really would be one. One could also call the same chair an aeroplane: I only have to add a propeller, wings and an engine. And yet I admit I should find it difficult to call it a lump of chewing gum or barley sugar, even if barley sugar shaped like a chair really existed. So one can say that everything is didactic, that everything — even the a-social — is social, for nothing human can exist outside society just as nothing can exist outside the cosmos. (This is not understood by those sociologists who believe only in society and ignore the cosmos from which they keep us separate.) And that everything is psychological. And that everything is number, mathematifiable, etc. . . .

And yet we have postmen, policemen, Zouaves, professors, poets. The professor is by his very function essentially didactic. If you wanted to turn a poet into a professor he would no longer be a poet, he would be a professor. If poets and poetry exist, it is doubtless because a poet is something different from a professor and gives us something different from a lesson. *Oedipus Rex* can teach us that if we infringe the moral laws (even involuntarily and then what is the use of the lesson?) the most awful things may happen to us. But if this tragedy is successful it is because it is a story that has been imagined, a fiction of such power that we believe in it and suffer *with* the characters: because it is a whole world that owes its existence to the creative imagination of the Ancient poet; because its heroes are alive; because this invented world fits into the real world and itself becomes real, although it never had any real existence and might never have been born. It was gratuitously created (do not tease me about the world 'gratuitously') — freely, if you prefer.

And yet at the same time this work is also testimony: having perhaps some basis in reality, but going beyond it, bringing it to life, transfiguring it. It is 'testimony' delivered through 'fiction': perhaps in art there is no deep contradiction between testimony and imagination.

Creative imagination is revelation. Like a lucid dream. We can never really be accused of lying. Everyone lies in his own way and that particular way expresses him.

A teacher is not a witness. He is a judge. Judge and party to the case. He does not use his imagination either.

Didacticism is above all an attitude of mind and an expression of the will to dominate.

Isn't Bérenger a character that makes your audience no longer ashamed to accept themselves and doesn't the resistance of Bérenger therefore mean the surrender of Ionesco? Why is this?

Right. Let us admit that you have caught me in the act of contradiction and that I have been tempted to write 'committed drama', to plead a cause and prosecute. But we all contradict ourselves more or less in life. The most eminent philosophers contradict themselves within the body of their system. But what of the poet, who creates first one work and then another? I do not believe we need overcome and resolve contradictions. That would mean impoverishment. We must allow contradictions to develop freely; perhaps our conflicts will resolve themselves dynamically by counter-balancing each other. We will see what that can lead to.

I may at one time write free and gratuitous drama; then *Tueur sans gages* and *Rhinocéros:* but even there I am not passing judgement, I am telling a story that happened to Bérenger; and I solicit interpretations (which I may perhaps not accept). I don't pass judgement? Perhaps, after all, I do. To plead a cause is also to have passed judgement: and in this case I think that Bérenger, my hero in *Rhinocéros*, is precisely (as J. P. Sartre so well expressed in the interview he gave you) one of those men who 'in an oppressive society, in its political form a dictatorship to which everyone seems to consent, bear witness to the opinion of those who do *not* consent: it is then that the worst dangers are avoided' That seems to me to be Bérenger all right.

Anyway Bérenger is I hope, above all a character. And if he is time resistant, it will be because he has proved himself as a character; he should, if he has any real worth, survive even after his 'message' has become outdated. Poetically, it is not his thought but his passion and his imaginative life that will matter, for his message could quite as well be delivered now by a journalist, a philosopher or a moralist etc. . . . The interest we may take to-day in a particular attitude, in spite of its human importance, takes second place to the permanent importance of art.

How is it then that you do not give up art itself?

Give up art? Can I, in spite of my pessimism and my bad temper, give up breathing? Poetry, the need to imagine and create, is as fundamental as the need to breathe. To breathe is to live and not to escape from life. Is one deserting if one composes a sonata? And what use is that sonata? What use is a painting? Is a non-representational picture (or even a representational one) making a practical stand? It is a social phenomenon, of course; but not practical.

Artistic creation answers a very necessary and imperative need of the mind.

People who are deprived of this satisfaction, people who are refused the freedom to play and invent and create works of art, regardless of 'commitment', suffer profoundly. Even if they are not at once clearly aware of it.

I know some of them. We must stop them being stifled.

Cahiers libres de la jeunesse, 1960.

INTERVIEW WITH EDITH MORA

In December 1949 *at* 6 *o'clock in the afternoon at the* Théâtre des Noctambules, *a very young company acted before a public as limited in numbers as it was well-informed the play of an unknown author:* La Cantatrice Chauve. *Some muttered between their laughter: 'He's a genius!'; others icily left the theatre.*

Ten years later the former Odéon *now the young* Théâtre de

France *opened by the President of the Republic, announces for the month of January the latest play of this same Ionesco,* Rhinocéros, *which has just been a triumphant success in Germany. So what new secret recipe for laughter has the author of* Les Chaises, La Leçon *and* Tueur sans gages *discovered, the author of those comedies which some have called 'anti-plays'?*

Laughter . . . laughter . . ., certainly I cannot say I do not try to arouse laughter; however, that is not my most important object! Laughter is merely the by-product of a dramatic conflict that one sees on the stage — or that one does *not* see if the play is a comedy, but then it is still implied — and laughter comes as a reprieve: we laugh so as not to cry . . .

And yet you really do have characters that are amusing in themselves, simply in their behaviour?

Some of them are at times comic because they invite derision, but they do not know it. All of them in any case are comically ridiculous: such as Amédée in *Comment s'en débarrasser?* and all the characters in *La Cantatrice Chauve*; if the latter are comic it is perhaps because they are dehumanised, emptied of all psychological content, because they have no internal dramatic conflict; whereas others, on the contrary, are comic because the way they behave as humans is ridiculous: like the characters in *Victimes du devoir* or the old couple in *Les Chaises*.

Like Bérenger also in Tueur sans gages?

He is touching, hardly comic; what is comic springs from his naïvety.

And is he the same in Rhinocéros, *where we find him again?*

There he is comic at the start, but the comic in him is finally submerged.

In my plays the comic is often merely a stage in the dramatic construction, and even a method of constructing the play. It becomes more and more of a tool, used to counter-point the dramatic action; this is obvious, I believe, in *La Leçon*.

So we could reach a definition of the comic which would be entirely your own?

Yes ... I think it is another aspect of the tragic.

Is it not fairly close to caricature like Jarry's, or in the style of Jarry?

Yes, in *La Cantatrice Chauve* I was close to Jarry, but later I have gone further away from him. You can find this kind of ... grotesqueness (after all this word would do) in Ghelderode, whom I'm very fond of; but with him there is a great ex-uberance of language, which I do not possess at all.

But is it not also and already the comic of an Arnolphe, of a George Dandin?

Ah! Molière! Of course, he is a master for all of us — in spite of his realism . . . But when these older writers use the comic and mix it with the tragic, in the end their characters are no longer funny: it is the tragic that comes out on top. In my plays it is just the opposite: they start by being comic, are tragic for a moment and end up in comedy or tragi-comedy.

But your own starting-point, what inspires you to write, is it the tragic or the comic?

I do not know, it is very difficult to dissociate them. And yet perhaps after all it is the comic; and then, as I follow my characters, in a way I become emotionally attached to them and the comedy becomes dramatic; but then I switch round and return to my starting-point. This must be apparent in *Amédée*. But it is not always like this and in my last two plays it is just the reverse.

Perhaps you are in the process of changing?

Perhaps, at this very moment. But I do not know what is going to happen to me tomorrow!

Well then, tell me what happened to you yesterday! How did you become an author . . . shall we say a comic author?

Right! Now you're in for the whole story! At seventeen I wrote poems that were a strange mixture of Maeterlinck and Francis Jammes, with a few surrealist touches . . .

Surrealism dazzled you? Liberated you?

Yes, perhaps, but I fully realised that liberation can come only when there is a genuine appreciation of what has been revealed and the ability to control these revelations from the supra-conscious world. I believe there must be in a writer, and even in a dramatist, a mixture of spontaneity, unawareness and lucidity; a lucidity unafraid of what spontaneous imagination may contribute. If lucidity is required of him, *a priori*, it is as though one shut the floodgates. We must first let the torrent rush in, and only then comes choice, control, grasp comprehension. But, I repeat, I do not have this lucidity when I start writing. What I think about my own drama is not programmatic, but the result of experience in my work.

Forgive me for coming back to surrealism, but you are, I believe, considered by the great surviving surrealists as the most successful practitioner of surrealism — Philippe Soupault told me this recently.

When he and Breton and Benjamin Péret saw my plays in 1952 and 53 they did indeed say to me: 'That's what *we* wanted to do!' But I have never belonged to their group, or to the neo-surrealists, although the movement has interested me. Anyway, I think I can explain why we have only just recently arrived at surrealist drama: the theatre is always twenty or thirty years behind poetry and even the cinema is in advance of the theatre.

In the theatre any mildly daring experiment is immediately condemned by hidebound criticism and mundane realism and then by authors and audiences fearing to give free rein to the forces of imagination . . . One dare not do in the theatre what after all can be done only in the theatre!

That is what you said this summer at the Congress of the International Theatre Institute at Helsinki?

Yes, in the theatre one can do anything, an author has extraordinary opportunities for unleashing his imagination: and no-one dares! People want the theatre to do everything, even to educate — or to re-educate, an inferior substitute then taking the place of thought (and you know what re-education leads to . . .). There are philosophers who write for the theatre, and their drama, instead of originating in a mode of expression proper to the theatre, is nothing but the discursive, unpoetical and undramatic expression of an ideology. Now drama and ideology ought to move in two parallel lines; drama should never be its slave. The playwright may have his universe, but it is one that can only be expressed in a theatrical idiom, just as music can only be expressed in music and painting in painting.

And how did you come to see that the theatre was the right medium for you?

I realised this was my natural way, my own personal mode of expression. When I manage to detach myself from the world and feel able to take a good look at it, it seems to me to be comic in its improbability.

You don't follow the fashion and speak of its . . . absurdity?

Exactly, it is far too fashionable. And then the absurd is conceived as being in some way an intrinsic part of existence. Now for me, intrinsically, everything that exists is logical, there is nothing absurd about it. It is the consciousness of being and existing that is astonishing . . . And I believe I am a comic writer thanks to this faculty, not only for observation, but for detachment, for being able to stand outside myself. When I go and see my doctor, for example, he is always amazed I can describe my symptoms to him like a physician and not like the patient I really am . . . And this saves me from 'self-pity-itis'.

Are you then sometimes the 'patient' at the same time as the physician, or rather the surgeon, in your comedies?

Oh! I have always made fun of myself in my writing! It must however, be admitted that this happens far less often now and that I take myself more and more seriously when I talk about what I do . . . In the end I fall into a kind of trap. But perhaps the fact that I denounce myself, as I do at this moment, will free me from the trap, after all?

You have just mentioned your writings: do you write anything else but plays?

Yes and no. I have written three short stories, tragi-comic and rather fantastic like my drama, which have become three plays: *Amédée*, then *Tueur sans gages* and *Rhinocéros*. It was after they had been written that I realised they were in fact written just like short plays.

You have just quoted the titles of your last two plays, the ones you said were notably different from the preceding ones. Is that not a sign that your conception of the theatre is changing?

On reflection I think I must admit that these last two plays are perhaps really, in spite of myself, a little less purely theatrical and rather more literary than the others. In writing them I have perhaps made certain concessions . . . *Rhinocéros* is a short story I have adapted for the stage; it tells a story, whereas normally what interests me above all in the theatre is *theatrical form*. A real play for me is more likely to be a formal structure than a story: there is a kind of dramatic progression in which the stages of development are different states of mind that increase in density.

Is this density not fatal to what is comic?

Yes, when it prevents the author from turning against himself, which must be an unbreakable rule for anyone who wants to be comic. One must not allow oneself to get bogged down in sentimentality. One needs to be somehow cruel and sardonic with oneself. What is most difficult is not to get too attached to oneself or one's characters — and yet continue to like them. One has to be able to regard them with a lucidity that is not malevolent but ironical. When an author gets too involved in one of his own characters, that character is a bad one. I have seen authors weeping at the first night of their plays and muttering: 'It's sublime! . . .'

But what if the character is particularly moving?

He should not be, not entirely. He must be as comic as he is moving, as distressing as he is ridiculous. Besides, one cannot pull perfect characters out of oneself, for an author is not perfect: he is a fool, like the rest of mankind!

(*Les Nouvelles littéraires, 1960.*)

FRAGMENTS OF AN ANSWER TO AN ENQUIRY

I am not very sure how I came to enter the theatre. It is impossible for me to give you more precise details on this subject. All I can tell you is that I have never tried to illustrate an ideology: or indicate the path of salvation to my contemporaries. If our planet is to-day in mortal danger, it is because we have had too many saviours: saviours hate humanity, because they cannot accept it. Doubtless I must have felt at some particular moment the need to produce a creative work. Already at the age of twelve I had written a play and a film scenario, which I have since lost. Later, I was taken up with other things, with what one calls life. Much later, I recovered not my first play but the desire or the need to write others. The need to invent and imagine is innate in man. We have all written or tried to write, paint, act, compose music, or at least build rabbit hutches — the fact that they are of practical use is nothing more than a pretext, just as faith simply furnishes a motive for the raising of cathedrals.

People who never reach the point of building a work of art, or even a straight piece of walling, spend their lives dreaming, lying or acting to themselves.

The free development of the powers of imagination must not be restricted. There must be no canalisation, no directives, no preconceived ideas, no limits. I believe a genuine work of art is one in which the initial intentions of the artist have been surpassed; where the flood of imagination has swept through the barriers or out of the narrow channels in which he first tried to confine it: extending beyond messages, ideologies and the desire to prove or to teach. This absolute freedom of the imagination is called escape or evasion by the gloomy critics of our time, whereas it is true creation. To make a new world is to satisfy the insistent demands of a mind that would be stifled if its needs were not fulfilled. Man is perhaps, as has been said, a laughing animal. Where there is no humour, there is no humanity; where there is no humour (self-detachment, taking liberties with oneself) there is a concentration camp. But man is above all a creative animal.

I probably wrote for the theatre, after trying to write other things, because at that moment I must have felt that drama was the supreme art, allowing the most complex materialisation of our profound need to create new worlds.

No. The public's reactions have had no influence on me. It is the *public* in the end that have got used to *me*; they support me (for the moment). I have never paid attention to the public.

And yet perhaps I have. I rather have the impression I have fought them; but they have never held it against me. Works of art are often imposed by force.

I have not paid attention to the critics either. Favourable or unfavourable. I mean I have not paid attention to them in my creative work. Hostile critics have, however, caused me a lot of trouble personally. Perhaps I am vain, but I can't help thinking my offerings have gone over the heads of some of my 'intellectual' critics. They can encourage people to come to the theatre or discourage them: it is in this way only that they have caused me trouble. I have made fun of them. But above all they have irritated me. They have been of no use whatsoever. They have really been a frightful nuisance: three or four of them have tried to make my plays their own, using them as weapons in support of their own ideology. I have refused to be their slave. They have not forgiven me. Some years ago they informed me that my drama was a blind alley, that I had a limited public of snobs, that I was dead. Recently they announced my death again, because I had reached a larger public. The merest hint of freedom or audacity, humour, fun and caricature all get on their nerves. (And even if the wit is not very subtle and the play only partially successful, why be so angry about it?) When in the end they get used to an approach you have succeeded in imposing upon them over a period of years, they are put out by the slightest change in this attitude; nothing must blur the image they have made for themselves.

They lack adaptability, good humour and often good faith.

I believe certain critics are responsible for bad drama and what is called 'the crisis in the theatre'. They stand for routine and fanaticism: whether it be reactionary, avant-garde or 'revolutionary' routine or fanaticism.

To take things too seriously is to build prisons, to be inquisitorial, didactic or boring, to make wars and to kill. I am well aware that we are not living in a period of great art. Our minds are in a strait-jacket. But why does one go to the theatre if its is not for 'play-acting'?

Yes. If I had not been 'successful' I should still have gone on writing for the theatre. It had become indispensable to me. Besides, success often comes through a misunderstanding, it is failure in disguise.

You ask me whether the theatre is an art that entertains or stimulates reflection? I have never understood that kind of question or the distinction made. I don't deny that the theatre changes with language and custom. The history of art is, of course, nothing but the history of its expression. Yes, there is something that changes and something that cannot change: and that is why the Noh plays, Sophocles' tragedies and Shakespeare's dramas are the kind of theatre that can be understood by men everywhere. The mechanics of the theatre can be modified, the essential laws of the theatre are unchanging. The same spirit pervades its various manifestations. Pre-Columbian art speaks to us now. There is nothing more contemporary than a Greek column.

Drama clearly reflects the anxiety of our present period. Nothing can prevent it being also the expression of an anxiety felt at all times. People died of love a hundred years ago, and also from the fear of death: they still do to-day.

These anxieties find clearer expression, they are more genuine, more complex, more profound, when they are fired by the power of the imagination. The less fettered and bound we are by the prejudices and other alienations we have tried to impose upon ourselves, by the restrictive desire to demonstrate this or that, the richer our creative work will be in manifold meaning. The more contradictory a piece of evidence is, the truer it is. We are told that to belong to our own times we ought to join some party or other. This limits us and falsifies our essential truth. 'Commitment', as it is now understood, is a catastrophe. Perhaps it is good to choose and be militant about something in practical life. But it is all the more necessary, if we are not to suffocate, to have complete freedom in creation, to open the doors and the windows to the fresh air of imagination; it is indispensable to be able to dream. When one tries to belong to one's own period, it usually happens that one belongs to no period at all. Any uniform, unilateral or partisan view is an expression of bad faith. There are many signposts in history. Naturally we carry within us the anxieties of our own epoch. An artist should allow them expression quite freely and naturally: when they contain their own lively contradictions they will reveal to us a complex and astonishing truth that is far more instructive than any lesson: lessons are given in order to lead us by the nose and conceal from us the complexity of truth and all its contradictions.

The lesson the theatre has to teach extends far beyond the giving of lessons.

IN THE LONG RUN I AM FOR CLASSICISM[1]

In your last play, L'Impromptu de l'Alma, *which Jacques Mauclair is rehearsing at the moment at the* Studio des Champs-Elysées, *you clearly take up the cudgels with certain 'doctors' among the Parisian critics. Can you tell us what you think about the function of criticism and of critics in general?*

Where criticism is concerned I have no standards. I destroyed my own standards. Once upon a time I was a critic myself. I wrote a series of articles about a great poet from a foreign country. Step by step I took his work to pieces, in order to show that it had no value. These articles gave rise to much polemical discussion. Then, some weeks later, I wrote a fresh series of articles in order to prove that this poet had written nothing but masterpieces. After this, no-one ever took me seriously as a critic. And yet can one be more serious or more honest? Read the dramatic critics consistently and see how most of them contradict themselves from one year to the next. I only speeded things up a little: with me, the contradictions were almost simultaneous. In reality, one proves whatever one wants to prove, everything is decided in advance. Criticism is as changeable as atmospheric conditions. Criticism does not really affect a work of art, though it seems to owe its very existence to what others think about it. If a critic has any authority, people think what he thinks or wants to believe. A critic is great when you can take him at his word. If he writes in good faith, he is not so changeable as the others in what he thinks he believes.

Once an opinion has been declared, one inevitably feels a

[1]A written answer to questions asked by *Bref*, which appeared with certain modifications in the number dated 15th February 1956. I here give the original text, without the changes made for publication.

need or temptation to think and say the opposite. An honest critic ought to write two contradictory articles about each work. This would reveal as much about criticism as about the process of human thought. It would also be revealing about the work itself. *L'Impromptu de l'Alma* is a rather wicked joke. I put on the stage friends like Barthes, Dort, etc. . . . To a large extent this play is a *montage* of quotations and complications drawn from their erudite studies: it is they who wrote the play. There is also another character that is Jean Jacques Gautier. I have not made a success of this character, but in spite of his verbal ferocity I don't hold this against him. And yet he is the most dangerous of dramatic critics: not because of his intelligence, for he is not intelligent; nor because of his severity for which there is no foundation; but because one knows, when he attacks an author, the latter is ready to believe himself a genius.

There is perhaps one possible way of writing criticism: to come to terms with a work through its own idiom and mythology, to accept this new universe and take stock of it. To say whether it really is what it makes out to be: to let the work speak for itself, or describe it and say exactly *what* it is and not what the critic would *like* it to be.

So perhaps the only valid standard of criticism is one based on appraisal of the work's expression. Expression is both form and content at the same time. When there is novelty in the expression, this is a sign of merit. To renew expression is to destroy clichés, an idiom that no longer has any significance; to renew expression is the result of a further effort to communicate the incommunicable. And this perhaps is the principal aim of art: to restore the virginity of an idiom. It is through the idiom of the cliché that one degrades certain essential realities which have lost their freshness and have to be discovered anew, just as buried towns are dug up from the sand.

Tell us how the creative process works with you. What do you think about your own drama?

Creation implies total liberty. It is an entirely different procedure from that involved in conceptual thought. There are two ways of knowing: logical, and aesthetic or intuitive. (I am quoting Croce.) When I write a play, I have no idea what it is going to be like. I have my ideas *afterwards*. At the start, there is nothing but an emotional state. *L'Impromptu de l'Alma* is an exception. For me art means the revelation of certain things that reason, everyday habits of thought, conceal from me. Art pierces everyday reality. It springs from a different state of mind.

Do you not have certain themes?

I call them obsessions, or anxieties. They are the same for everyone. Art is only possible because it is founded on this identity, this universality of response. Of course there are also the obsessions of the *petit-bourgeois*, which Barthes wants to try and analyse. The fear of being petit-bourgeois is an obsession of petit-bourgeois 'intellectuals'. But these obsessions are above all personal to him: it is he who is the petit-bourgeois. Dort reproaches me for limiting my plays to the world of the family. This is true of only a few of my plays, and after all the world of the family *does* exist: if Bernard Dort does not know it, that does not prevent it being as important as our internal world or the collective world of the community, which is the most external to us. In this totalitarian world, where people are only comrades and no longer friends, a revolt will spring up which will, I hope, restore man's inner life, his real humanity, his freedom and equilibrium.

The world of the family is in fact a community, society on a small scale. There is as much or more to be found inside us as outside. For me, boulevard theatre and political drama are simply entertainment.

But Dort did not accuse you of writing boulevard theatre...

For me, any drama dealing with secondary problems (social or triangular, stories about other people) is drama that diverts. In 'The Fist' Kafka recounts the story of some people who wanted to build a Tower of Babel and who stopped at the second floor because the solution of problems arising from the building of the Tower (housing the personnel, the constitution of trade unions, allocation of jobs etc...) had become the principal objective. They had forgotten they were meant to be constructing the Tower. They had forgotten their *goal*. The only thing that counts is my conflict with the universe. The universe is my obstacle.

Your drama, then, takes up an aggressive and provoking attitude to the audience and the world?

I suppose so, I don't do it deliberately.

Besides, your first plays were a kind of 'anti-theatre'.

They were in fact a criticism of the commonplace, a parody of a kind of theatre that was no longer 'theatre'. Clearly, what I discovered in my conversation manuals was a criticism of 'hollow' language, slogans and fixed ideas. The petit-bourgeois is for me a man of fixed ideas, one who turns up at every period in every society: a conformist, a man who adopts the thought-patterns (or the principal ideology) of whatever society he happens to belong to and stops asking questions. An average man who turns up everywhere.

In the end I realised I did not really want to write 'anti-theatre' but 'theatre'. I hope I have rediscovered intuitively in

E*

my own mind the permanent basic outlines of drama. In the long run I am all for classicism: that is what the 'avant-garde' is. The discovery of forgotten archetypes, changeless but expressed in a new way: any true creative artist is classical . . . the *petit-bourgeois* is the person who has forgotten the archetype and is absorbed in the stereotype. The archetype is always young.

What productions in Paris have impressed you most in the last ten years?

I can hardly think of any. But I could mention Shakespeare, Molière, Racine, and recently, Marivaux, and Kleist. I have little knowledge of the younger authors. I did not like Oscar Wilde's *Ideal Husband*, he is too much a prisoner of his own time, expressing nothing but his own time; a work of art should embrace the transient and the intransient.

You are not much interested in the others?

I myself *am* the others, essentially my problems can only be the same as other people's. I am like everyone else. Whether one likes it or not, one *is* everyone else. But 'everyone else' does not always realise this.

Are you sure that in your drama there are no moral preoccupations, no . . . educative tendencies?

By being subjective . . . I believe I am writing drama that is objective. Perhaps I am socially-minded in spite of myself.

Now tell us something about Les Chaises. *Tell us for example about the part played by props in* Les Chaises?

They express the proliferation of material things. The obtrusive presence of objects expresses spiritual absence. The world seems to me at times too massive and heavy, at others too light, insubstantial, evanescent, imponderable.

Do you identify yourself with some of the characters in your plays?

With me every play springs from a kind of self-analysis . . .
. . . *exhibitionism?* . . .

No. For the *me* I try to 'exhibit' is a *me* that is *us* . . . Of course, one has to try and reach this universal *me* and set him free. The world within can be as rich as the world without. Both of them, moreover, are only two aspects of the same reality.

The fact that your plays are acted far from the Left Bank, in Belgium, Holland, Switzerland, Germany, Finland, Sweden, Argentina, England and Canada, the fact that Saul Steinberg illustrates them in the United States and that Buñuel is doing Jacques *in Mexico proves perhaps that they do after all answer some special need of our own period. And as we are talking about the way your plays are being performed abroad, tell us what you think about a 'popular' theatre that would be accessible to a new public of people who at the moment do not go to the theatre?*

That is a question for the great captains of the theatre. As for me I think my drama is very simple, very easy to understand, visual, primitive, childish. It is simply a question of getting rid of certain rationalistic mental habits. On the other hand I do not think it is necessary to make a systematic distinction between '*popular*' *theatre* and '*bourgeois*' *theatre*, for these two notions need not be mutually exclusive. The petit-bourgeois mind can be found, as I have already told you, in every class of society. I do not believe either in drama that is prophetic and carries a 'message'. To present a thesis is to intrude rational intentions into something of a quite different nature. Authors have always wanted to make propaganda. The great ones are those who have failed.

Do you think your drama belongs to any particular movement, that it is a link in some chain of evolution?

That is not for me to say. If it has any value it should assist in
the destruction and renewal of modes of expression. I am trying
to rediscover tradition, but I am not being academic. Just the
reverse.

I could say that my drama is a drama of derision. But it is not
any particular society that seems to me derisory. It is man. So
you see there are some eternal themes.

I do not know whether a drama or a comedy is more compel-
ling than a symphony or a painting. What I do know is that
it is far more difficult for theatre to be theatre than for music to
be music. Music is a direct reflection of its own times, yet it is
also timeless. The proof that it belongs to its own age lies in its
continued evolution: it always reflects the stylistic cross-
currents of its period. But also, like all the arts, people can
understand it across the centuries. It is not only that the songs
of the Middle Ages, Bach, Beethoven, Wagner, Mozart,
Stravinsky, Schönberg, Bartok and Webern do not cancel one
another out, but they go to make up the variety found in the
unity of music. Music has this advantage, that it has been best
able to ignore the rigours of the state and political dictatorship:
it has escaped tyranny. Life has been easier for painters too: if
they were painting the portrait of a king or cardinal or some
court lady, painters just painted, regardless of their subject. The
theatre has been much less free, much more a prisoner of its
own age, much more closely watched by the powers-that-be;
and, though this may seem paradoxical, if art is too much the
prisoner of a political regime, it has less chance of expressing
not only universality but also its own age. A whole period

cannot be summed up by a political system or some particular ideology. It is for this reason, being less free, that it has been much harder for the theatre to go its own way: this is very noticeable to-day, especially in totalitarian regimes.

One can express the world we call 'the external world', while appearing only to look inside oneself: just as one can quite well express the world 'within', while appearing to talk about other people.

It is the job of the philosophers to explain and find illumination in works of art.

I dislike Brecht just because he is didactic and ideological. He is not primitive, he is elementary. He is not simple, he is simplistic. He does not give us matter for thought, he is himself the reflection and illustration of an ideology, he teaches me nothing, he is useless repetition. Brechtian man, moreover, is flat, he has only two dimensions, surface dimensions, he is merely social: what he lacks is dimension in depth, metaphysical dimension. Brechtian man is incomplete and often he is merely a puppet. Thus in *The Exception and the Rule* or in *Man for Man*, Brecht's human beings are conditioned solely by social factors, interpreted, moreover in one particular way. There is another side to us too, which goes beyond the social and gives us a certain freedom in relation to society. Whether it is really a question of freedom or a more complex conditioning of human beings is another problem. In any case Brechtian man is crippled, for his author denies him his deepest inner reality; he is bogus, for he is alienated from what truly determines him. There is no theatre if no secret is revealed; there is no art without metaphysics, and there is no society away from its non-social context.

Beckett is essentially tragic. Tragic, because with him it is precisely the whole of the human condition which comes into play and not man in this or that society, or man seen through and distorted by a particular ideology that both simplifies and mutilates his historical and metaphysical reality, the authentic reality into which man is integrated. Whether one is pessimistic or optimistic is another question. What is true and important is that man should appear in all his deeper aspects and various dimensions. Beckett poses the problem of the ultimate ends of man; the picture of history and the human condition this author gives us is more complex, more soundly based.

Obviously the theatre cannot shut its eyes to society. But for Brecht there is only one social problem: the struggle of the classes. In reality, this is only one aspect of the social world. After all, my relations with my neighbour are still social relations. The relations between a married couple or a pair of lovers are also social relations. As man is not alone, everything is naturally social. We can talk of the sociology of marriage, of neighbourhood or factory life, the sociology, alas, of concentration camps, or of religious communities, of school or military life, or the sociology of work: which all means that social problems and conflicts are not purely *class* problems. So to reduce all the problems of society to this is to belittle both society and mankind.

Really it is *political* drama that is insufficiently social; it is dehumanised, as it offers us only a limited view of social and human reality, a prejudiced view.

What obsesses me personally, what interests me profoundly, what I am committed to is the problem of the human condition as a whole, in its social and non-social aspects. It is in its non-social aspect that man is profoundly alone. Faced with death, for example. Then society no longer counts. Or when, say, I awake to myself and the world, and suddenly gain or regain an awareness that I *am*, that I exist, that I am surrounded by something, all sorts of objects, a sort of world, and everything seems strange and incomprehensible to me and I am overwhelmed by the wonder of being alive. I steep myself in wonder. Then the universe seems to me infinitely strange and foreign. At such a moment I gaze upon it with a mixture of anguish and euphoria; separate from the universe, as though placed at a certain distance outside it; I look and I see pictures, creatures that move in a kind of timeless time and spaceless space, emitting sounds that are a kind of language I no longer understand or ever register. 'What is all this?' I wonder, 'what does it all mean?', and out of this state of mind, which seems to spring from the most fundamental part of my nature, is strangely born at times a feeling that everything is comic and derisory, at others a feeling of despair that the world should be so utterly ephemeral and precarious, as if it all existed and did not exist at one and the same time, as if it lay somewhere between being and not being: and that is the origin of my tragic farces, *Les Chaises*, for example, in which I myself would find it difficult to say whether some of the characters exist or not, whether the real is truer than the unreal or the reverse.

For me, it is as though at every moment the actual world had completely lost its actuality. As though there were nothing there; as though there were no foundations for anything or as though it escaped us. Only one thing, however, is vividly present: the constant tearing of the veil of appearances; the constant destruction of everything in construction. Nothing holds together, everything falls apart. But I am merely repeating the words of King Solomon: all is vanity, all things return to dust, all is shifting shadow-play. I can see no other truth. It is King Solomon who is my master.

Now how does all this become drama, I mean how is all this translated into action? I do not know.

At the start it all seems more like a linguistic idiom than action, since it springs from a lyrical state of mind. And yet at the same time characters or phantoms appear, which move on the stage speaking this language and having adventures. They speak of what they feel, they act according to their feelings.

But the theatre has its own idiom: a language of words and gestures and objects, action itself, for everything tends to expression and meaning. Everything is language. A language that attempts to reveal what lies outside history, perhaps even to integrate this into history.

PORTRAITS

PORTRAIT OF CARAGIALE[1]
1852-1912

Born in 1852, just outside Bucharest, I. L. Caragiale wrote excellent short stories and a few plays that 'revolutionised' the Rumanian theatre, which was easy enough to revolutionise as one might say it hardly existed. In fact he created it. To judge by the quality of his comedies of character and manners, written unfortunately in a language that has no world-wide currency, I. L. Caragiale is probably the greatest of the unknown dramatists. Having sharpened his disgust of the society of his time by denigrating it throughout his work, justifiably and violently, with talent and humour, I. L. Caragiale took advantage of a belated inheritance to expatriate himself towards the end of his life to Berlin, where he died in 1912 aged 60 years and 5 months.

In the January of the same year he had refused to return to Bucharest for the few days allotted to the *official* celebration of his career and his sixtieth birthday—yes, his compatriots had come to admire him for insulting them for so long.

In his work I. L. Caragiale lashed out at business interests, the civil service and politicians: his grievances were well-founded, naturally.

In his youth I. L. Caragiale had frequented a conservative political and literary club, under whose auspices he published his

<hr>

[1]A play by this author, *La Lettre perdue*, was acted in Paris in 1955 at the *Théatre de Poche* in a production by Marcel Cuvelier. (It appeared in the collection *'Les hommes célèbres'*, 3rd volume, edited by G. Mazenod.)

first two comedies (*A Stormy Night* and *Leonida faced with reaction*) performed respectively in 1879 and 1880, so some people tried to see in this author an enemy of liberalism and democracy. This was only partly true. Later, Caragiale was an intimate friend of the creator of the Rumanian socialist movement and joined in socialist demonstrations. In his most important comedy (*Lost Letter*, played in 1883), I. L. Caragiale, objective in his vehemence, attacked conservatives and liberals alike. This gave others the opportunity to discover socialist sympathies and revolutionary tendencies in his work. This is perhaps more true, for the excellent reason that as no socialist government existed there was no point in attacking it. Starting with the men of his own age, Caragiale is really a critic of all men and any society. What is peculiarly his own is the exceptional virulence of his criticism. Indeed mankind, as it is presented to us by this author, does not seem to deserve to exist. His characters are samples of humanity so degraded that they leave us with no hope. A world in which all is base and derisory can only give rise to the purest and most pitiless comedy.

Caragiale's chief originality is that all his characters are imbeciles. Imagine Henry Monnier's little people more minutely characterised, sinking completely into the irrationality of the cretin. These social anthropoids are vain and grasping: without intelligence, they are on the other hand amazingly cunning; they want to 'arrive'; they are the heirs and beneficiaries of those revolutionaries, heroes, luminaries and philosophers who have convulsed the world with their ideas; they are the result of this convulsion.   Well, someone has to get something out of it.   What is depressing is that the ideas themselves, seen through this intellectual fog, are degraded and lose all significance, so that in the end everything is compromised, both men and ideologies. Caragiale does not take things lightly and is far removed from a Feydeau, though he does have the latter's genius for construction, or from a Labiche, though they may have some affinity with regard to formal technique. Endowed with the spirit of naturalism, it is from the world of everyday life that he chose his characters, but he has revealed them to us in their deepest essence. He made of them models and types: there was no denying they existed. Everyone could see the country's government ministers in the prevaricating Prefect of *The Lost Letter*; the waffling members of parliament in the conservative barrister of the play; the muddle-headed journalists in the poet of *The Stormy Night*; the small investors in the father, Leonida.

If we examine things more closely, and first of all in their regional context, they look even worse. Emerging from the Middle Ages of the Balkans, which had stretched on into the middle of the last century in the provinces of Rumania, the country suddenly staggered straight into liberal Europe. Rapid reforms gave the nation a new social structure; a bourgeois class sprang up from nowhere; the '*petit-bourgeois*' appeared, a tradesman wearing the uniform of a civic guard, identical to his French colleague and the universal '*petit-bourgeois*', but still more stupid. As for the upper ranks of the *bourgeoisie* they hardly seemed any different from the lower. Their ignorance was more complex. Understanding nothing about historical evolution, even the least fortunate of these worthy citizens still had a kind of ambition to understand something, but without success: Caragiale shows us this mental effort too, collapsing under the strain, in all its distressing glory.

Caragiale's heroes are mad about politics. They are political cretins. To such an extent that they have deformed their most everday speech. The whole population feeds on the newspapers: written by idiots, they are read by idiots. The distortion of language, the obsession with politics is so great that all life's actions are bathed in a bizarre eloquence consisting of expressions as high-sounding as they are miraculously inept, gathered from an inexhaustible storehouse of the most arrant nonsense, which serves as a noble justification for actions that are unspeakable: friends are betrayed 'in the interests of the party'; deceived by her lover, a woman throws vitriol at his face, because 'she has a republican temperament'; an anonymous denunciation is 'signed courageously' and sent to the conservative minister; some become forgers for the good of their country; and members of parliament for love of 'our dear little country'; people subscribe to any political regime, because they are 'impartial'; posts are awarded only to 'the sons of the Nation'; a shady character deserves consideration 'because he is one of us'; only the Nations's children 'have the right to be decorated, for decorations are made with the sweat of the people'; 'all those who devour the people' must be sent to prison; an insignificant local revolt 'is a great example for the whole of Europe, which has its eyes fixed upon us'; a Prefect who refuses a parliamentary candidate his support is 'drinking the blood of the people'; 'the Pope is no fool, although he's a Jesuit'; Leonida wants 'a government that would pay all its citizens a good monthly pension and forbid you to pay taxes'. Then there are these great principles: 'I like treason, but I hate traitors', 'a nation that does not move forward stays where it is' and 'all nations have their bankrupts, Rumania too must have hers'.

The gap that exists between a language as obscure as it is elevated and the low cunning of the characters, their cere-

monious politeness and their fundamental dishonesty, together with the grotesque adultery, finally take this drama far
beyond naturalism, for it becomes absurdly fantastic. Never
touched by any feeling of guilt, any idea of sacrifice, or in
fact by any ideas at all ('as we already have heads, what good
would intelligence do us?' Caragiale asks ironically), these
characters, amazingly untroubled by conscience, are about
the meanest to be found anywhere in literature. So Caragiale
arrives at a criticism of society unequalled in its ferocity.

In the end one realises that Caragiale is fighting not against
the principles of the new institutions, but against the bad
faith of those who represent them, the governing hyprocrisy
and the unspeakable stupidity of the bourgeois, all causes of
the breakdown, as if by sabotage, of the democratic machine
before it had had a chance to get going, and of the decay of
the new society before it had had time to mature; everything
crumbles into chaos. I. L. Caragiale does not tell us that the
previous society was better. He does not believe it. He thinks
'society' is like this. Everything has always to be remade
afresh. The author washes his hands of it (*he always denied
his interest in anything but art for art's sake*), and he retired abroad,
where he never had the chance to get to know people well
enough for them to become as unbearable as those he had
known only too well at home.

INTRODUCTION TO THREE AUTHORS

Humour is liberty. We need humour and fantasy[1]; and 'respectable' people have banished them from the theatre and
contemporary literature, where we find either the worldly
spirit of the boulevard or the sordid 'literature' of commitment.

[1]Translator's note: *cocasserie*.

This absence of humour, this ferocious commitment has been characteristic of our attitude for some time now. Hitler did not allow humour; Maurras put the 'political' first; a Stalinist bourgeois, in Russia or in the West, has no sense of it and forbids the imagination to be imaginative, by that I mean free and truth-revealing in its freedom; realism is rampant, a limited realism, reduced to such a narrow plane of reality and so falsified by fanaticism that it is nothing but sheer unreality; we are trapped and immobilised by Sartrisms, in the chains and dungeons of a commitment that was meant to bring freedom. All these 'commitments' of yesterday and to-day have already led and could still lead straight into the concentration camps of the most varied and antagonistic fanatical doctrines, or to the physical and intellectual supremacy of regimes whose apparent differences and antagonisms merely mask their profoundly identical nature, the same 'serious' spirit.

Humour brings us a free and lucid realisation of the tragic or derisory condition of man; there can be no truth unless we allow full play to the intelligence, and this can be governed only by an artist who is not screened off from reality by ready-made ideas and ideologies and thus alone is able to establish direct and therefore genuine contact with this reality.

The three plays published in this number of *Avant-Scène* (*Les trois Chapeaux-claque*, by Mihura, *Sur une plage de l'ouest* by Carlos Larra, and *Le Naufrage ou Miss Ann Saunders* by Simone Dubreuilh) have this advantage: that they combine humour with tragedy and profound truth with fantasy[1], which, as one of the principles of caricature, underlines and sets off the truth of things by making it larger than life. The 'irrational' style of these plays can show up aberrant contradictions,

[1] Translator's note: *le cocasse*.

stupidity and absurdity far better than formal rationalism or mechanical dialectics. Fancy is revealing; everything imagined is true; nothing is true if it is not imagined. As far as humour is concerned, it is not only the one valid critical approach, the very spirit of criticism: it also provides—in direct contrast to systematised thinking, which in the name of *realism* leads us on into a frozen dream that is an escape, a flight from reality—the only opportunity we have of detaching ourselves from our tragi-comic human condition or the sickness of living; assuming of course it has been recognised, assimilated and experienced. To become fully conscious of the atrocious and to laugh at it is to master the atrocious. Those who do not know how to laugh, who are born with blank minds, whose vocation it is to live as prisoners and for whom rage and murder are the only means of release are the killers of this world, who exclude friendship, love and noble feelings in order to keep the bad ones: hate and fury.

'Demystification' is much talked about nowadays; unfortunately the demystifiers replace one set of taboos by anti-taboo taboos, which become far more restricting than the old ones. So demystifiers do nothing but mystify us, enslave us, and provide us with a rigid vocabulary, a new language that blinds and deceives.

There is only one true way of demystifying: by means of humour, especially if it is 'black'; logic is revealed by our awareness of the illogicality of the absurd; laughter alone respects no taboo and prevents the setting-up of new taboos that are anti-taboo; the comic alone is able to give us the strength to bear the tragedy of existence. The authentic nature of things, the truth, can only be revealed to us through fancy, which is more realistic than all our realisms.

The three little plays of Mihura, Simone Dubreuilh and Carlos Larra require the audience or the reader to make a little effort and to have some mental adaptability: to grasp the rational through the irrational; to pass from one plane of reality to another; from life to dream; from dream to life. Only apparently disjointed, they are fundamentally an excellent exercise if we wish to enrich dramatic expression, to multiply and vary those areas of 'reality' we hand over to the prospecting genius of a dramatist. These three plays also link pleasantry with the atrocious, buffoonery with distress, and gravity with derision. They provide a very useful exercise in intellectual gymnastics.

(*L'Avant-Scène*, 15th February 1959.)

AN ADDRESS DELIVERED TO A GATHERING OF FRENCH AND GERMAN WRITERS

Why and for whom does one write? If one writes a letter, a speech, a lesson or a petition, it is in order to express ideas or feelings to someone, to request, to teach, to convince, to protest, etc. The aim of the business of writing lies outside itself. Writing is a means. We write *to* other people, *for* other people.

I could also write something intended to prove, convince or teach, etc., and I could call this letter, manifesto or speech which I have written a poem, a comedy or a tragedy, etc. What I would in fact have produced is a letter, sermon or petition and not a poem or a play, etc. . . .

Again, I may want to write a letter or petition, and in spite of myself it may turn out to be a poem; a lecture with illustrations that turns into a comedy or perhaps a tragedy: the secret, unconscious intentions of a creative artist may not coincide exactly with his superficial or apparent intentions.

An architect builds a temple, a palace or a small house. A musician composes a symphony. The architect tells us this is for the faithful to have a place made for prayer; for the King to have a dwelling spacious enough to house distinguished guests, various dignitaries and countless soldiers; and for the peasant to have somewhere to shelter his family and his pig.

And the symphony, the musician will tell us, 'expresses my feelings'; it is a kind of language.

But the architect is properly caught out: the faithful have died and religion is in ruins, but the temple is not, it is still standing; and generation after generation come to admire the abandoned temple, the empty palace and the picturesque old house, which now shelters only furniture or memories.

As for the symphony, it is above all the way it is composed that excites connoisseurs of music; the composer's little feelings have died with him.

The building and the symphony now reveal nothing but the laws of architecture or the principles that govern the moving architecture of music. The essence of a building and a symphony having found its purest expression, they have come into their own.

What then is this temple or that symphony? They are quite simply structures. I do not even need to know that this building is a place of prayer; its intended use matters little, is irrelevant, neither subtracts nor adds anything and has no effect on whether it stands or falls: the essential characteristic of a building is simply that it is something built. Besides, this temple is only a temple because I wanted it to be one; but if I refuse to see it as a temple, I cannot refuse to see it as a building. It may or may not serve some purpose. But it does not need to serve a purpose in order to be a building: to be a building it does not need a congregation. One may even regret it should serve no purpose, at times like these when there are so few Christian churches; but it can still be turned into a barracks or a garage.

And so we see this temple could in fact be a Christian church, a barracks, a garage, a hospital, a lunatic asylum or a hall for political meetings, etc. . . . I could also pull it down.

But apart from being a church, a place of amusement or a stable or a Communist party headquarters or an academy for 'distanciationists,' this temple is first and foremost a construction that obeys the laws of construction, it has a reality of its own.

A play too is a construction of the imagination, which should also stand entirely in its own right; its essential nature should be such that it cannot be confused with a novel written in dialogue, or with a sermon, a lesson, a speech or an ode; for if it could, it would no longer be a play but a lesson, a speech or a sermon, etc. . . . from which it could hardly be distinguished. A play can only be precisely this and no more: different from all those other things, which are *not* plays.

If a building constructed for the faithful has no need of the faithful to be a building just the same, if it does not need a congregation—neither does a play need an audience to be a play.

And yet a play has been written *for* a public, for the public of its own time; it cannot be conceived without reference to the audience it is aimed at.

But there is no certainty even about that, whatever the author himself may often say, for his authenticity as a creative artist can be measured by the extent to which his own work eludes him, just as sons liberate themselves from their father's control and escape from them.

The work of art asks to be born, just as a child asks to be born. It springs from the depths of the soul. A child is not born for society's sake, although society claims him. He is born for the sake of being born. A work of art too is born for the sake of being born, it imposes itself on its author, it demands existence without asking or considering whether society has called for it or not. Obviously, society can also claim a work of art and use it as it likes: it can condemn it or destroy it. A work of art may or may not fulfil a social function, but it is not equivalent to this social function; its essence is supra-social.

A play is just like a symphony or a building: simply a

monument, a living world. It is a combination of situations, words and characters, a dynamic construction with its own logic, form and unity; the resultant of equally balanced internal forces that conflict but cohere.

Of course I shall be told that the characters in a play, who are an incarnation of the antagonisms without which there can be no theatre, talk about something, express passions, ideas and even ideologies, that they belong to their own time and reflect it, that they make a stand for or against something. But all this is merely the material of drama, material out of which a dramatic monument is built, just as stone is only the material used in a piece of architecture. Can it be objected that a dramatic work thus conceived is an illusion or of little use? In the same way one might also call a building an illusion, a sonata an illusion or of no practical use. What is the purpose then of this play? Its purpose is to be a play. Just as the purpose of a sonata is to be a sonata. So a work of art answers the need to produce a creative work. A play answers the need to create characters, to present the passions in flesh and blood. The world thus created is not an image of the world; it is made *in* the image of the world.

As for me, as long as I can remember I have always wanted to write poems or short stories or plays. I have always been haunted by worlds I wanted to bring into the world; when I was twelve I really did write for no-one, but out of the sheer need to write. Or I wrote for myself. Later still, for quite a long time, I would have written even in the desert.

Subsequently, like everybody else, I wrote in order to say something, to express myself, to defend certain things or to attack them. I actually used to believe that was why I was writing. But I was wrong. That was only the starting point, the initial impulse. To bring characters to life, to give palpable form to figments of the imagination, this was the secret reason I had to write.

Again I shall be told that I have a particular background, that I live in a certain historical context of time, that I can only belong to my own period. That language has a history, so history must exist. That I am participating in one moment of history. That the French I write is not mediaeval French, that contemporary music is very different from the music of Lulli, that non-representational painting did not exist in the Sixteenth Century. But this does not mean that I am a prisoner of my own times, that I can or should address myself only to an audience of my own times. I do not know what this audience is. We only know ourselves. In fact a work of art springs from a particular soil, a particular time, a particular society; it springs from them, but it does not grow in the same direction; it does not turn back to them. We must not confuse the point of departure with the point of arrival.

And so a work of art really is above all an adventure of the mind.

And if it is absolutely necessary that art or the theatre should have a purpose, I shall say it ought to remind people that there are some activities which serve no useful purpose and that it is imperative such things should be. For this is the theatre: the construction of a machine that moves, the universe on show, seen as a spectacle, man at one and the same time being spectacle and spectator. And this too is the new and 'useless' *free* theatre we need so much, a theatre that is truly free (for the 'free theatre' of Antoine was the opposite of free).

But nowadays people are scared stiff both of freedom and

of humour; they do not realise that life is impossible without freedom and humour, that the simplest gesture and the slightest effort require the full deployment of our powers of imagination; and they try, stupidly and desperately, to shackle and imprison us within the blind walls of the narrowest kind of realism, calling it life when it is really death, and light of day when it is really the shades of night. I maintain that the world is not audacious enough, and that is why we suffer. And I also maintain that it is not our monotonous everday lives but our dreams and imagination that call for audacity, that contain and reveal essential and fundamental truths. And I would even add (to make a concession to those who believe only in practical utility) that if aeroplanes now furrow the sky it is because we dreamed of flight before we made ourselves wings. It is because we dreamed of flying that it has proved possible to fly. And flying in itself is quite useless. It was only after the event that we demonstrated or invented the necessity for flying, as though to gloss over its utter and essential uselessness. A uselessness which, however, fulfilled a need. Difficult to get anyone to admit this, I know.

Just watch people hurrying busily through the streets. They seem preoccupied, look neither left nor right, but have their eyes fixed on the ground like dogs. They rush straight ahead, but always without looking where they are going, for they are mechanically covering a well-known route, mapped out in advance. It is exactly the same in all the great cities of the world. Modern, universal man is man in a hurry, he has no time, he is a prisoner of necessity, he does not understand that a thing need have no use; nor does he understand that fundamentally it is the useful thing that can become a useless and overwhelming burden. If one cannot understand the usefulness of the useless and the uselessness of the useful, one cannot understand art; and a country in which art is not understood is a country of slaves and robots, a country of unhappy people who neither laugh nor smile, a country without mind or spirit; where there is no humour, where there is no laughter, there is anger and hatred. For these busy, anxious people, hurtling towards some goal which is not a human goal or is simply a mirage, may quite suddenly answer some clarion call, respond to the voice of some devil or madman and succumb to some delirious fanaticism, some wild collective madness or other, some hysteria that sweeps the masses. Forms of rhinoceritis of every kind, from left and right, are there to threaten humanity when men have no time to think or collect themselves; and they lie in wait for mankind today, because we have lost all feeling and taste for genuine solitude. For solitude is not *separation* but *meditation*, and we know that social groups, it has been said already, are most often a collection of solitary human beings. No-one ever talked of 'incommunicability' at a time when men were able to isolate themselves; incommunicability and isolation are paradoxically the tragic themes of the modern world, where everything is done collectively, where there is constant nationalisation or socialisation, where man can no longer be alone—for even in 'individualistic' countries the individual conscience is in fact invaded and destroyed by the pressure of the crushing and impersonal world of slogans: whether good or bad, for politics or publicity, it is all odious propaganda, the sickness of our time. The intelligence is so corrupted by it that no-one understands when an author refuses to commit himself to serve under the flag of one of our prevalent ideologies—when in other words he refuses to surrender.

Moreover, even if audiences insist they can find a certain lesson in a play, it will still be the least important thing they could have found. And what is there in a play that is more important than a lesson? That is easy: the action, things that start happening, get ravelled and unravelled, and then stop happening.

It is not the wisdom or the moral of La Fontaine's fables that still interests us now—for it is the eternal elementary wisdom of common sense—but rather the way it is brought to life, used as material for a linguistic idiom and transformed into a miraculous mythology. This is art: the miraculous brought to life. And this above all is what the theatre should be.

In Europe as in America it is under sentence of death, because it is this no longer.

Commercialism and 'realism' are killing the theatre, they do not give it life. For unaudacious theatre—the ready-made drama of Broadway and the Boulevards, as well as realistic drama, strapped into the strait-jacket of time-worn theses—is fundamentally unrealistic theatre: bourgeois unreality on the one hand, so-called socialist unreality on the other—these are the great dangers that threaten the theatre and art, the power of imagination and the living and creative force of the human mind.

(February 1960.)

TESTIMONY

WHEN I WRITE . . .

When I write I do not worry whether 'I am being avant-garde or not', whether or not I am 'an avant-garde author'. I try to say how the world appears to me, what it seems to me to be, as honestly as I can, without a thought for propaganda, with no intention of guiding the conscience of my contemporaries; within the limits of my own subjectivity I try to be an objective witness. As I am writing for the theatre I am only concerned with personifying and incarnating a sense of reality which is both comic and tragic. Putting the characters I imagine onto the stage — and for me they are real, as real as they are imaginary—is something that happens naturally or not at all. If you want or do not want to be avant-garde before you start writing, if you deliberately choose or reject an avant-garde approach, you are, as a creative artist, putting the cart before the horse, you are evading the truth that lies within you and missing the point, you are acting in bad faith. I am what I am, take it or leave it. Genuine self-examination is most successful when it helps you to be yourself. And it is by being completely oneself that one has the best chance of being other people too.

When I was a boy I used to live near Vaugirard Square. And I remember—how long ago now!—that ill-lit street one autumn or winter evening: my mother was holding me by the hand and I was frightened, as children often are; we were shopping for the evening meal. Dark shapes were flitting along the pavements, people hurrying by: hallucinating ghost-like shadows. When memory brings back a picture of that street, when I think that almost all those people are now dead, everything does indeed seem to me to be shadow and evanescence. My head spins with anguish. Really, that *is* the world: a desert of fading shadows. How can revolutions change anything at all? The tyrants are dead, but so are the master-minds who succeeded them. The world is something else too; I was still a child when, soon after I arrived in my second country, I saw a fairly young man, tall and strong, beating and kicking an old man. Both of them are dead now too.

I have no other pictures of the world apart from those which express evanescence, and callousness, vanity and anger, emptiness, or hideous useless hate. Everything has merely confirmed what I had seen and understood in my childhood: futile and sordid fits of rage, cries suddenly blanketed by the silence, shadows swallowed up for ever by the night. What else have I to say?

Obviously it's not very original. It has been said thousands of times. But a child had discovered it for himself, before he learnt it from so many others, who therefore simply confirmed his childhood vision. It matters little to me whether this vision is or is not surrealist, naturalist, expressionist, decadent, romantic or socialist. It is enough for me to think of it as perfectly realistic, for reality is rooted in the unreal. Is it not true that we are going to die?

It will be said that this view of the world and of death is *petit-bourgeois*. Are children *petits-bourgeois* so soon? Perhaps. I find this vision of the world in a great number of '*petits bourgeois*' throughout the centuries: in Solomon, that *petit-bourgeois* King; in Buddha, that *petit-bourgeois* prince; in those *petits-bourgeois*, Shakespeare and St. John of the Cross;

and in a great many more *petits-bourgeois*, saints, peasants, townsfolk, philosophers, believers, atheists etc. . . .

I notice too that this same age-old and enduring 'vision' of life and death is also modern or contemporary: when we read Proust we can catch a great feeling for the uncertainty of existence, which permeates his world of love and memory, of phantoms decked with lace; in Flaubert's *L'Education sentimentale* do we not see an illustration of man destroyed by time, a time in which everything comes to nought, in which everything crumbles against the roar of revolution and a shifting background of societies overthrown and reconstructed and overthrown again? And do we not become aware of almost the same thing in Brecht's *Mother Courage?* This is a play attacking war, of course, but this is not its main theme: time erodes and kills, we are shown this in time of war, but this only makes it more violent and more blatant, the pace of destruction is quickened; fundamentally it is not about the destruction of man by war but rather the destruction of man by time, by the fact of living.

Is not the theme of many of Chekov's plays also the theme of evanescence? It is not principally the death-agony of society that I see in *The Cherry Orchard* or *The Three Sisters* but rather, through one particular society, the destiny of all men and all societies.

In all these authors one can see diverse situations, various countries, different periods and conflicting ideologies, but all these particular situations are simply a series of happenings in time, which again and again show me one and the same situation, one eternal event in conditions that change, like the varied expression of one invariable thought.

I do not refute the possibility of a different attitude of mind; I am not opposed to the hopes of Teilhard de Chardin's disciples or those of the Marxists, but I think I can claim that a work of art must express one or other of our fundamental attitudes, that it is nothing if it does not go beyond the ephemeral truths or obsessions of history, if it is held back by this or that fashion—whether it be symbolist, naturalist, surrealist or social realist—and fails to attain a universality that is positive and profound.

So the avant-garde is nothing but a topical historical expression of an event of timeless topicality (if I can put it thus), of a supra-historical reality. The importance of Beckett's *End Game*, for example, consists in the fact that it is closer to the Book of Job than to the plays of the Boulevards or to the *chansonniers*. Across the ages and the ephemeral fashions of History this work has rediscovered a less ephemeral type-history, a primordial situation which all the rest follow.

What is called 'avant-garde' is interesting only if it is a return to sources, if it rejoins a living tradition by cutting through a hidebound academic traditionalism that has been rejected.

To belong to one's own time, all that is needed is a certain awareness, a sincerity that is blind and therefore clairvoyant: either one does belong (through one's idiom), or one does not, and it happens almost instinctively. One has the impression too that the more one belongs to one's own age, the more one belongs to every age (once the crust of superficial contemporaneity has been broken). Every genuine creative artist makes an effort to get rid of the relics and clichés of a worn-out idiom, in order to rediscover one that is simplified, reduced to essentials and renascent, capable of expressing realities old and new, topical and timeless, alive and permanent, both particular and universal.

The freshest and newest works of art can easily be recognised, they speak to every age. Yes, the leader I follow is King Solomon; and Job, that contemporary of Beckett.

(April 1958, *In answer to an Investigation, Lettres françaises*)

I HAVE NEVER QUITE SUCCEEDED

I have never quite succeeded in getting used to existence, whether it be the existence of the world or of other people, or above all of myself. Sometimes it seems to me that the forms of life are suddenly emptied of their contents, reality is unreal, words are nothing but sounds bereft of sense, these houses and this sky are no longer anything but façades concealing nothing, people appear to be moving about automatically and without reason; everything seems to melt into thin air, everything is threatened—myself included—by a silent and imminent collapse into I know not what abyss, where there is no more night or day. What magic power still holds it all together? And what does it all mean, this appearance of movement, this appearance of light, these sorts of objects, this sort of world? And yet here I am, surrounded by the halo of creation, unable to embrace these insubstantial shades, lost to understanding, out of my element, cut off from something undefinable without which everything spells deprivation. I examine myself and see myself invaded by inconceivable distress, by nameless regrets and inexplicable remorse, by a kind of love, by a kind of hate, by a semblance of joy, by a strange pity (for what? for whom?); I see myself torn apart by blind forces rising from my innermost self and clashing in some desperate unresolved conflict; and it seems I can identify myself with one or other of these, although I know quite well I am not entirely this one or that one (what do they want from me?), for it is clear I can never know who I am, or why I am.

No event, no magical occurrence surprises me, no new train of thought excites me (no interest in culture), not a single thing ever seems to me stranger than another, for everything is evened out and blurred by the all-embracing strangeness and improbability of the universe. The very idea that we exist and can express ourselves seems to me incongruous. Those who do not share my belief that the fact of existence is unthinkable, may find in accepting existence that only a part of it is intrinsically sensible and logical, right or wrong. Whereas for me, the whole idea of existence being inconceivable, anything that actually exists seems intrinsically possible. No private frontiers, for me, can separate the real from the unreal, the true from the false, I have no standards, no references. I feel that I am there, on the fringe of existence, a stranger to the march of history, not at all 'with it', bemused, paralysed into a state of primordial stupefaction. The gates are closed to me, or perhaps they have all disappeared together with the walls and all sense of distinction.

Doubtless what I have just said describes my state of mind only when it has reached the most complete moment of truth. In spite of everything, I am still alive. And I even manage to write . . . plays for example. You even do me the honour of asking me what I think I believe about the theatre. So what I have said up to now may seem irrelevant to the subject. I do in fact feel convinced that I have spoken of nothing else, that I have never strayed from the heart of the matter. However, whether this be true or not, the theatre, like literature or any other manifestation of cultural life, has an only limited interest for me, only partially affects me; I do not really attribute much value to what is communicable, or rather to what has been communicated already, to anything extraneous, to the passage of events, to deeds or doing.

For me the theatre—my own drama—is usually a confession; I do nothing but make admissions (incomprehensible to the deaf, that is inevitable), for what else can I do? I try to project onto the stage an inner drama (incomprehensible to myself) and tell myself that in any case, the microcosm being a small-scale reproduction of the macrocosm, it may happen that this tattered and disjointed inner world is in some way a reflection or a symbol of universal disruption. So there is no plot, no architectural construction, no puzzles to be solved, only the inscrutable enigma of the unknown; no real characters, just people without identity (at any moment they may contradict their own nature or perhaps one will change places with another) simply a sequence of events without sequence, a series of fortuitous incidents unlinked by cause and effect, inexplicable adventures, emotional states, an indescribable tangle, but alive with intentions, impulses and discordant passions, steeped in contradiction. This may appear tragic or comic or both at the same time, for I am incapable of distinguishing one from the other. I want only to render my own strange and improbable universe.

Perhaps, however, I could make a certain distinction: when I gaze attentively, from the outside, at what seems to appear before me, from which I am completely detached, then the insubstantial texture of creation, the behaviour of those human creatures and their languages—which I just seem able to make out and which is for me hermetic or empty and as though *arbitrarily invented*—all their activities, everything falls apart, becomes nonsensical, infallibly turns to derision and is transformed into a bitter burlesque. It is out of this existential vacuum that my comedies can then be born.

But when, on the other hand, one lets one's own apparitions blossom into life, still faintly coloured with dark traces of passions as violent as they are incoherent, one knows that in their vehemence these rival forces will tear at one another and give birth to drama.

And so I do after all feel myself carried away by the mobility of drama. But as stories are never interesting, I long to rediscover the basic and purest principles of the theatre, and to reproduce them in pure scenic movement.

(Arts, 1953)

HE WHO DARES NOT TO HATE BECOMES A TRAITOR

In the Pasternak Affair, one terrible thing strikes me forcibly. Pasternak has been accused by the official writers of his country of being a renegade, a traitor, a bad patriot and a man filled with hatred. Why? Quite simply because he has had and expressed the feeling that the people confronting him, his adversaries, were after all human beings too, as human as their enemies and that, like the others, they had a right to pity, respect, understanding and even love. This is the way things are: when you love, you are accused of hating; when your heart is full of hate, you are congratulated because, they say, 'you love'.

In fact, it seems nowadays that one is forbidden not to hate; all charity is banned. So the worst fault is to give way 'to the temptation of goodness'.

I have never been able to look upon my adversary as an

obscene reptile; if I could, I would feel that *I* was an obscene reptile hating another obscene reptile. Or perhaps I should say he runs no risk of turning into an obscene reptile unless *he* considers I *am* an obscene reptile. Each time I make some declaration or defend some point of view, I am tempted to believe that the opposing point of view is more justified or just as justified as my own.

I have not got a partisan mind. If there is one thing I detest it is the partisan spirit: often to such an extent that in detesting hatred I become full of hate myself, and start playing hatred's game. Is it a weakness to say that everyone and no-one is right? To welcome other people's opinions more willingly or as willingly as one's own? Does it show some intellectual inferiority not to have a categorical and partial attitude? Not to restrict oneself to shibboleths and doctrines and passionately held beliefs that are quite rigid and pre-determined, that totally justify one's actions and one's resentments, canalise one's anger and give free rein to the will to kill? The savagery of revenge or 'just' retribution is out of all proportion to its 'rational' aims.

It seems to me that in our own time and at all times religions and ideologies are not and never have been anything but alibis, pretexts that mask the murderous will, the destructive instinct, the fundamental aggressiveness and the profound hatred that man employs against man; people have killed to protect Order and to oppose Order, to defend God and to attack God, for their country's sake, to break up an Order that is evil, to free themselves from God, to throw off a foreign yoke, to liberate others, to punish the wicked for the sake of the race, to bring stability back to the world, for the sanity of the human race, for glory or because we all have to live and snatch our bread from the hands of others: people have tortured and massacred above all in the name of Love and Charity. In the name of social justice! The saviours of mankind have founded inquisitions, invented concentration camps, constructed crematory ovens, established tyrannies. The guardians of society have built prisons, the enemies of society commit murder: I even believe the prisons appeared before the crimes.

I shall be saying nothing new if I declare that I am afraid of those who yearn for the salvation or the happiness of mankind When I see a sanctimonious man, I take to my heels as if he were a criminal lunatic armed with a dagger. 'We have to choose', we shall be told nowadays. 'We have to choose the lesser evil. It is better not to go against history': but which way is history going? I believe this is a new deception, a new ideological justification for the same constant impulse to kill: for this way 'one commits oneself', and one has a more subtle reason for compromise or for joining this or that party of assassins. This is the latest hypocrisy in the most recent of mystifications. We have seen it at work: he who dares *not* to hate is outlawed by society: he becomes a traitor, a pariah.

And yet my play, *Tueur sans gages*, was written well before the Pasternak Affair, which in my view only confirms once more what I had tried to show in that piece.

But are we not all moving towards death? Death is really the end, the goal of all existence. Death does not have to be buttressed by any ideology. To live is to die and to kill: every creature defends itself by killing, kills to live. In this hatred of man for man (who really needs a doctrine that allows him to kill with a clear conscience), in this inborn instinct for crime (political, patriotic, religious etc.) is there not something like an underlying hatred of the very condition of man?

Do we perhaps feel in a confused sort of way, regardless of ideology, that we cannot help being, at one and the same time, both killer and killed, governor and governed, the instrument and the victim of all-conquering death? ...

... And yet, and yet we are *here*. It could be there is some reason, which escapes our reason, for existence: that too is possible.

(*Arts*, the 3rd of March 1959,
Advance notice for *Tueur sans gages*)

MY PLAYS AND I

All my plays have their origin in two fundamental states of consciousness: now the one, now the other is predominant, and sometimes they are combined. These basic states of consciousness are an awareness of evanescence and of solidity, of emptiness and of too much presence, of the unreal transparency of the world and its opacity, of light and of thick darkness. Each of us has surely felt at moments that the substance of the world is dream-like, that the walls are no longer solid, that we seem to be able to see through everything into a spaceless universe made up of pure light and colour; at such a moment the whole of life, the whole history of the world, becomes useless, senseless and impossible. When you fail to go beyond this first stage of *dépaysement* — for you really do have the impression you are waking to a world unknown — the sensation of evanescence gives you a feeling of anguish, a form of giddiness. But all this may equally well lead to euphoria: the anguish suddenly turns into release; nothing counts now except the wonder of being, that new and amazing consciousness of life in the glow of a fresh dawn, when we have found our freedom again; the fact of being astonishes us, in a world that now seems all illusion and pretence, in which all human behaviour tells of absurdity and all history of absolute futility; all reality and all language appear to lose their articulation, to disintegrate and collapse, so what possible reaction is there left, when everything has ceased to matter, but to laugh at it all? I myself at one such moment felt so completely free, so released, that I had the impression I could do anything I wished with the language and the people of a world that no longer seemed to me anything but a baseless and ridiculous sham.

Of course this state of consciousness is very rare; this joy and wonder at being alive, in a universe that troubles me no more and *is* no more, can only just hold; more commonly the opposite feeling prevails: what is light grows heavy, the transparent becomes dense, the world oppresses, the universe is crushing me. A curtain, an impassable wall stands between me and the world, between me and myself; matter fills every corner, takes up all the space and its weight annihilates all freedom; the horizon closes in and the world becomes a stifling dungeon. Language breaks down in a different way and words drop like stones or dead bodies; I feel I am invaded by heavy forces, against which I can only fight a losing battle.

This was definitely the starting point of those of my plays that are generally considered the more dramatic: *Amédée* and *Victimes du devoir*. Given such a state of mind, words, their magic gone, are obviously replaced by objects, by properties: countless mushrooms sprout in the flat of Amédée and Madeleine; a dead body suffering from 'geometrical progression' grows there too and turns the tenants out; in *Victimes du devoir*, when coffee is to be served to three of the characters, there is a mounting pile of hundreds of cups; the furniture in *Le Nouveau*

Locataire first blocks up every staircase in the building, then clutters the stage, and finally entombs the character who came to take a room in the house; in *Les Chaises* the stage is filled with dozens of chairs for invisible guests; and in *Jacques* several noses appear on the face of a young girl. When words are worn out, the mind is worn out. The universe, encumbered with matter, is then empty of presence: 'too much' links up with 'not enough' and objects are the materialization of solitude, of the victory of the anti-spiritual forces, of everything we are struggling against. But in this anxious situation I do not quite give up the fight, and if, as I hope, I manage in spite of the anguish to introduce into the anguish, humour — which is a happy symptom of the other presence — this humour is my outlet, my release and my salvation.

I have no intention of passing judgment on my plays. It is not for me to do so. I have simply tried to give some indication of what emotional material went into their making, of what was at their source: a mood and not an ideology, an impulse not a programme; the cohesive unity that grants formal structure to emotions in their primitive state satisfies an inner need and does not answer the logic of some structural order imposed from without; not submission to some pre-determined action, but the exteriorisation of a dynamism of the psyche.

La Cantatrice Chauve is the only one of my plays the critics consider to be 'purely comic'. And yet there again the comic seems to me to be an expression of the unusual. But in my view the unusual can spring only from the dullest and most ordinary daily routine and from our everyday prose, when pursued beyond their limits. To feel the absurdity or improbability of everyday life and language is already to have transcended it; in order to transcend it, you must first saturate yourself in it. The comic is the unusual pure and simple; nothing surprises me more than banality; the 'surreal' is there, within our reach, in our daily conversation.

(Opening remarks from a talk given at Lausanne in
November 1954)

I HAVE OFTEN BEEN ASKED . . .

I have often been asked to say what my aims and intentions were in writing this or that play. When I was asked to explain *La Cantatrice Chauve*, for example, my first play, I said it was a parody of 'Boulevard' theatre or simply of the Theatre, a criticism of the verbal clichés and mechanical behaviour of people; I also said it was the expression of a feeling for the strangeness of everyday things, a strangeness that appears at the very heart of the most outworn commonplace; it was thought to be a criticism of the *petite bourgeoisie*, even in particular of the English middle classes, with whom moreover I had no acquaintance at all; it was thought to be an attempt to break down language or destroy the theatre; it was also thought to be abstract drama, since there is no plot in this play; it was thought to show the 'comic' in its purest form, or to be the invention of a new Labiche, using all the most traditional comic devices; it was called 'avant-garde', although no-one can agree on a definition of the word 'avant-garde', it was said to be 'pure theatre', although no-one knows exactly what 'pure theatre' is either.

If I myself say that it was a perfectly gratuitous game, I neither reject nor confirm the previous definitions or explanations, for even a playful play, perhaps above all a playful play, is loaded with all kinds of meanings, which emerge in the actual playing of the game. Really, in writing this play and those that followed, I never had one 'intention' at the start, but a multiplicity of half-conscious and half-unconscious intentions. Indeed, for me, it is thanks to and in the process of artistic creation that the intention (or intentions) becomes clear. Constructing a play is merely allowing its internal structure to emerge and stand revealed.

(*Arts*, 1955(?))

INTERLUDE

SCALES

First Series

—When you go walking in the park, eh? (Answer yes or no.)

—Well, I like that.

—The child arrives (when?)

—Don't ask so many questions.

—When I used to go to school.

—Thought: a concept is not what people think. It is something else. Which is quite different. Besides, I, for example, have one.

—How greedy we are.

—Well, you see.

—If a forest springs up to impede your progress, brush the trees aside. The brambles will follow you.

—It's six of one and half a dozen of the other, if I may so express myself.

—I like the spring and its diaphanous leaves; the summer and its weighty leaves. The autumn and the rusty leaves. The

174

winter and its non-existent leaves: that's because they are white. In fact, all the seasons, in fact, in fact, in fact. It's not so much the seasons, it's them, sorry, those trees.

—It's really something, I'm telling you.

—If you (yourself).

—I once had, begad, at home, I had.

—When I was a lad, every Thursday, as I live and breathe, when I was a lad, as I.

—Why, Madame?

—There is.

—On his head he had a felt hat, imagine that! Take it off. What's it matter to you do you *mind*? He flew into a temper come on don't be a silly sausage about what? I used to dance with duchesses gloved to the elbows the shoulders the breasts the shoulders the bellies the throat to cover it up because they were all stark naked; well then so what so what then well then so what; explain can't you that one's a real c . . .; if he's a c . . . there's no point; well then what then? Just a minute then *you* tell *me;* there's no point telling *you* you're no fool but you just ought to see things like everyone else; it's the instinct of observation (no, no, the other cries, leaping to the skies, observation has no instinct! and with that he collapsed).

—Ah, remember the permanent way, the railway bridge of

sighs, the poplars, no popular sales, the populace ails and cries, an aleless man of the people wails, lays his head on the rails and dies. What memories and none avails.

—Mother Peep's geese.

—Ssh! Reduce the ten-ton tenor's tones.

—Everyone has some: men, women and children. If they haven't any, you lend them some. Some would rather, others not. And even things, when they're useful; but not money. There's more than that in life. Space too, far from it.

—Advice: musn't (de)bunk.

Second Series

—When I was, I loved to ——— myself. People for your liver, my lad. It was an American tourist. I ordered some. Always unpopular! And yet, since Your Majesty willed it so, that's correct. Remain, my states, contradict me if I'm wrong.

—Just at that moment, the mob, at your service, on the war-path: oh Queen of frightful kings!... Beware.

—Whereas from down below, from up on high, from the very best, in vain, them and me, you led astray. In the West, at the start, the scenery was tooroolating. The Danegeld gave the business its distinguished side. The extinguisher appeared: one, two, three. Should I, after reflection, slow down, as I thought, or on the contrary give way? My ears, my fledgelings, *sine die*, were ringling. What's the latest news? The hydrocephalic and his swan-song; the green leaf and its camisole: irreducible by a third, all our feathered friends. The result was bad for his failure: about thirty bottles, aqueducts or other. Supremely chair, the melody. Of course, there's no doubt frippery foils the official. No brown decision was eaten without virtuous opposition. As always in the past.

—Toes, toes, what do you want me? Assassinate the blue Belgians, evacuate them from the spot, skimp the belly dance, put the toreador off his beat and the spinach on its guard? I don't want, no, I don't want. Compassion demands a fully rendered account. Winter is man, as well as the rest. Oh, toes, toes, what do you want me?

—Let's put a spurt on, Macedonia: the imaginative cramp-iron has immortalised the ative, the ative!

—The tart of the glade, the hedgehog's wear and tear, the discoveries of the Delaware, the oblisquity in the oesophagus the vertebra from behind, that's my triumph, that's my triumph!

OLYMPIA

Deprived of her support, Olympia was forfeit. Her fandango had never been stripped so bare. However, encumbered with cock-feather cares, she spiked the guns of war, brought Austria to a standstill and invited the gardener's derision. About every five pages, she nonchalantly neutralised nativity, well wrapped up for the beginners. Need was for cataplasms and like adventures!

'Fritters, fritters, darling little fritters!' she cried, tapping her pretty little sleeve and turning up her cheek.

'Delectabilities!' the improper onlookers approved. But can one do any better?

The three possibilities are worth a moment's hesitation. The compliment is delivered while the moments hesitate.

The compliment's deliverance is the delivery of a compliment to the moment. Hesitation is a compliment delivered to the three possibilities. The three possibilities hesitate between the three possible deliveries of the moment. The moments deliver compliments to the compliment. The compliments hesitate between the three possible compliments of the moment. Possibilities and compliments are all three hesitant.

The resistant hesitate. The hesitant resist.

3. MY PLAYS

La Cantatrice Chauve

In 1948, before writing my first play, *La Cantatrice Chauve*, I did not want to become a playwright. My only ambition was to learn English. Learning English does not necessarily lead to writing plays. In fact it was because I failed to learn English that I became a dramatist. Nor did I write these plays as a kind of revenge for my failure, although *La Cantatrice Chauve* has been called a satire on the English middle-classes. If I had tried and failed to learn Italian, Russian or Turkish, it would have been quite as easy to say that the play resulting from these vain efforts was a satire on Italian, Russian or Turkish society. I feel I should make myself clear. This is what happened: nine or ten years ago, in order to learn English, I bought an English-French Conversation Manual for Beginners. I set to work. I conscientiously copied out phrases from my manual in order to learn them by heart. Then I found, reading them over attentively, that I was learning not English but some very surprising truths: that there are seven days in the week, for example, which I happened to know before; or that the floor is below us, the ceiling above us, another thing that I may well have known before but had never thought seriously about or had forgotten, and suddenly it seemed to me as stupefying as it was indisputably true. I suppose I must have a fairly philosophical turn of mind to have noticed that these were not just simple English phrases with their French translation which I was copying into my exercise-book, but in fact fundamental truths and profound statements.

For all that, I had not yet reached the point of giving English up. And a good thing too, for after these universal truths the author of my manual passed on from the general to the particular; and in order to do so, he expressed himself, doubtless inspired by the Platonic method, in the form of dialogue. In the third lesson two characters were brought together and I still cannot tell whether they were real or invented: Mr and Mrs Smith, an English couple. To my great surprise Mrs Smith informed her husband that they had several children, that they lived in the outskirts of London, that their name was Smith, that Mr Smith worked in an office, that they had a maid called Mary, who was English too, that for twenty years they had known some friends called Martin, and that their home was a castle because 'An Englishman's home is his castle'.

Of course, I imagine Mr Smith must have been somewhat aware of all this; but you can never be sure, some people are so absent-minded; besides, it is good to remind our fellows of things they may be in danger of forgetting or take too much for granted. Apart from these particular eternal truths, there were other temporal truths which became clear: for example, that the Smiths had just dined and that, according to the clock, it was nine o'clock in the evening, English time.

Allow me to draw your attention to the nature of Mrs Smith's assertions, which are perfectly irrefutable truisms; and also to the positively Cartesian approach of the author of my English Manual, for it was his superlatively systematic pursuit of the truth which was so remarkable. In the fifth lesson the Martins, the Smiths' friends, arrived; the conversation was taken up by all four and more complex truths were built upon these elementary axioms: 'The country is more peaceful than big cities', some maintained; 'Yes, but cities are more highly populated and there are more shops', replied the others, which is equally true and proves, moreover, that contrasting truths can quite well coexist.

It was at that moment that I saw the light. I no longer wanted merely to improve my knowledge of the English language. If I had persisted in enlarging my English vocabulary, in learning words, simply in order to translate into another language what I could just as well say in French, without paying any attention to the matter contained in these words, in what they reveal, this would have meant falling into the sin of formalism, which those who nowadays direct our thinking so rightly condemn. I had become more ambitious: I wanted to communicate to my contemporaries the essential truths of which the manual of English-French conversation had made me aware. On the other hand the dialogue between the Smiths, the Martins, the Smiths *and* the Martins, was genuinely dramatic, for drama *is* dialogue. So what I had to produce was a play. Therefore I wrote *La Cantatrice Chauve*, which is thus a specifically didactic work for the theatre. And why is this work called *La Cantatrice Chauve* and not *L'Anglais sans Peine*, which I first thought of calling it, or *L'Heure Anglaise*, which is the title that occurred to me a little later? It would take too long to explain in full: one of the reasons why *La Cantatrice Chauve* received this title is that no prima donna, with or without hair, appears in the play. This detail should suffice. A whole section of the play is made by stringing together phrases taken from my English Manual; the Smiths and the Martins in the Manual are the Smiths and the Martins in my play, they are the same people, utter the same maxims, and perform the same actions or the same 'inactions'. In any 'didactic drama', it is not our business to be original, to say what we think ourselves: that would be a serious crime against objective *truth;* we have only, humbly, to pass on the knowledge which has itself been passed to us, the ideas we have been given. How could I have allowed myself to make the slightest change to words expressing in such an edifying manner the ultimate truth? As it was *genuinely* didactic, my play must on no account be original or demonstrate my own talent!

... However, the text of *La Cantatrice Chauve* only started off as a lesson (and a plagiarism). An extraordinary phenomenon took place, I know not how: before my very eyes the text underwent a subtle transformation, against my will. After a time, those inspired yet simple sentences which I had so painstakingly copied into my schoolboy's exercise-book, detached themselves from the pages on which they had been written, changed places all by themselves, became garbled and corrupted. Although I had copied them down so carefully, so correctly, one after the other, the lines of dialogue in the manual had got out of hand. It happened to dependable and undeniable truths such as 'the floor is below us, the ceiling above us'. An affirmation, as categorical as it is sound, such as: the seven days of the week are Monday, Tuesday, Wednesday, Thursday, Friday, Saturday, Sunday, so deteriorated that Mr Smith, my hero, informed us that the week was composed of three days, which were: Tuesday, Thursday and Tuesday. My characters, my *braves bourgeois*, the Martins, husband and wife, were stricken with amnesia: although seeing each other and speaking to each other every day, they no longer recognised each other. Other alarming things happened: the Smiths told us of the death of a certain Bobby Watson, impossible to identify, because they also told us that three quarters of the inhabitants of the town, men, women, children, cats and ideologists were all called Bobby Watson. Finally a fifth and unexpected character turned up to cause more trouble between the peaceable couples: the Captain of the Fire Brigade. And he told stories which seemed to be about a young bull that gave birth to an enormous heifer, a mouse that begot a mountain; then the fireman went off so as not to miss a fire that had been foreseen three days before, noted in his diary and due to break out at the other side of the town, while the Smiths and the Martins took up their conversation again. Unfortunately the wise and elementary truths they exchanged, when strung together, had gone mad, the language had become disjointed, the characters distorted; words, now absurd, had been emptied of their content and it all ended with a quarrel the cause of which it was impossible to discover, for my heroes and heroines hurled into one another's faces not lines of dialogue, not even scraps of sentences, not words, but syllables or consonants or vowels! . . .

. . . For me, what had happened was a kind of collapse of reality. The words had turned into sounding shells devoid of meaning; the characters too, of course, had been emptied of psychology and the world appeared to me in an unearthly, perhaps its true, light, beyond understanding and governed by arbitrary laws.

While writing this play (for it had become a kind of play or anti-play, that is to say a real parody of a play, a comedy of comedies), I had felt genuinely uneasy, sick and dizzy. Every now and then I had to stop working and, wondering what devil could be forcing me on to write, I would go and lie down on the sofa, afraid I might see it sinking into the abyss; and myself with it. When I had finished, I was nevertheless very proud of it. I imagined I had written something like the *tragedy of language*! . . . When it was acted, I was almost surprised to hear the laughter of the audience, who took it all (and still take it) quite happily, considering it a comedy all right, even a sort of rag. A few avoided this mistake (Jean Pouillon for example) and recognised a certain malaise. Others realised that I was poking fun at the theatre of Bernstein and his actors: Nicolas Bataille's cast had already realised this, when they had tried to act the play (especially during the first performances) as if it were a melodrama.

Later, serious critics and scholars analysed the work and interpreted it solely as a criticism of bourgeois society and a parody of Boulevard Theatre. I have just said that I accept this interpretation too: but to my mind there is no question of it being a satire of a *petit bourgeois* mentality that belongs to any particular society. It is above all about a kind of universal *petite bourgeoisie*, the *petit bourgeois* being a man of fixed ideas and slogans, a ubiquitous conformist: this conformism is, of course, revealed by the *mechanical language*. The text of *La Cantatrice Chauve*, or the Manual for learning English (or Russian or Portuguese), consisting as it did of ready-made expressions and the most threadbare clichés, revealed to me all that is automatic in the language and behaviour of people: 'talking for the sake of talking', talking because there is nothing personal to say, the absence of any life within, the mechanical routine of every-day life, man sunk in his social background, no longer able to distinguish himself from it. The Smiths and the Martins no longer know how to talk because they no longer know how to think, they no longer know how to think because they are no longer capable of being moved, they have no passions, they no longer know how to 'be', they can

'become' anyone or anything, for as they are no longer themselves, in an impersonal world, they can only be someone else,
they are inter-changeable: Martin can change places with
Smith and vice versa, no-one would notice the difference. A
tragic character does not change, he breaks up; he is himself,
he is *real*. Comic characters are people who do not exist.

(*The start of a talk given to French Institutes in Italy*, 1958)

CONCERNING *La Cantatrice Chauve* (DIARY)

10th April 1951
The theatre (or what is called theatre) taken to pieces.

La Cantatrice Chauve, like *La Leçon*, among other things attempts
to make the mechanics of drama function in a vacuum. An
experiment in abstract or non-representational drama. Or, on
the contrary, concrete drama if you like, since it consists only
of what can be seen, since it comes to life on the stage, since it
is play-acting, playing with words, with scenes and images,
giving concrete expression to symbols. And so made of non-
representational forms. The interest does not lie in any kind
of plot, in any particular 'action', which may play a subordinate
part, but must do no more than canalise a dramatic tension it
supports, sustains and punctuates. The aim is to release
dramatic tension without the help of any proper plot or any
special subject. But it still leads, in the end, to the revelation of
something monstrous: this is essential, moreover, for in the
last resort drama is a revelation of monstrosity or of some
monstrous formless state of being or of monstrous forms that
we carry within ourselves. The task is to arrive at this exaltation
or these revelations without a theme or subject that justifies or

motivates, for this would be ideological and so false and hypocritical.

The progression of purposeless passion, a rising crescendo that is all the more natural, dramatic and exciting because it is not hampered by content, and by that I mean any *apparent* content or subject which conceals the *genuine* subject from us: the particular meaning of a dramatic plot hides its essential significance.

Abstract theatre. Pure drama. Anti-thematic, anti-ideological, anti-social-realist, anti-philosophical, anti-boulevard-psychology, anti-bourgeois, the re-discovery of a new 'free' theatre. And by 'free' I mean liberated, without prejudice, exploratory: the only theatre that can be a sincere and precise witness and uncover fresh evidence.

La Cantatrice Chauve: characters without character. Puppets. Faceless creatures. Or rather empty frames, which the actors can fill with their own faces, their own shapes, souls, flesh and blood. Into the disconnected and meaningless words that they utter they can put what they like, express what they like: comedy, drama, humour, themselves, what they have in them that is more than themselves. They have no need to slip into the skins of their characters, into other people's skins, all they have to do is to slip straight into their own skins. This is not so easy as it looks. It is not so easy to be oneself, to play one's own character.

And yet the young cast of *La Cantatrice Chauve* really succeeded in being themselves. Or rather a part of themselves. Hollow, purely social characters: for there is no such thing as a social soul.

They were full of grace, the young actors in Nicolas Bataille's company in *La Cantatrice Chauve:* a void in Sunday-clothes, a charming void, a blossoming void, a void of phantom figures, a youthful void, a contemporary void. Beyond the emptiness, there still remained their charm.

Push burlesque to its extreme limits, then, with a flick of the finger, an imperceptible transition, and you are back in tragedy. It is a conjuring trick. The public should not notice the passage from burlesque to tragedy. Neither perhaps should the actors, or only slightly. The light changes. That is what I tried in *La Leçon*.

A burlesque text, play it dramatic.
A dramatic text, play it burlesque.
Make words say things they never meant.

One cannot always take credit for everything: an author's comic writing is very often the expression of a certain confusion. His own nonsense is exploited, it makes people laugh. It also makes many dramatic critics say that what one writes is extremely intelligent.

Every period has its own special commonplaces, apart from the more ordinary ones that belong to every period. Every ideology, I mean every ideological cliché will one day look pretty silly . . . and comical.

If I understood everything, I would obviously not be 'comic'.

THE BIRTH OF *La Cantatrice*

I never thought of this comedy as a true comedy. In fact it was only a parody of a play, a comedy of comedies. I used to read it to groups of friends, when they came to the house, to make them laugh. As they laughed quite heartily, I found there was a real comic force in the text. I realised later, when reading Raymond Queneau's *Exercices de style*, that my experiments in writing had a certain similarity with his own. Then Monique Saint-Come persuaded me that I had indeed written a kind of comic play; so I found the courage to leave my manuscript with her, and as she was doing production work with the youthful company of Nicolas Bataille, she showed the play to him. Nicolas Bataille and his actors, Paulette Frantz, Claude Mansard, Simone Mozet and Henri-Jacques Huet decided to start rehearsals immediately.

The title, however, had to be changed. I suggested *L'Heure anglaise*, *Big-Ben Folies*, *Une Heure d'Anglais* etc . . . Bataille rightly made me realise that the play could then be taken for a satire on the English. And this was not intended. No suitable title could be found. It was discovered by chance. Henri-Jacques Huet—who played the part of the Fireman so admirably—made a slip of the tongue during the final rehearsals. While delivering the monologue about the Cold, where there was some passing reference to an *'institutrice blonde'*, Henri-Jacques made a mistake and said *'cantatrice chauve'*. 'There's the title of the play!' I cried. So that is how *La Cantatrice Chauve* came to be called *La Cantatrice Chauve*.

It became apparent during the rehearsals that the play had movement; actions, although without action; rhythm and development, though plotless; and progression of an abstract kind.

A parody of drama is even more dramatic than straight drama, for it simply emphasises and exaggerates, like caricature, a characteristic line.

The text was played without cuts (except for Mr Smith's anecdote, which was mimed on the stage instead, although I restored it in the first volume of my published plays), until the closing scene, which was not played at all. After discussion we all agreed to drop the final scene. Indeed, it could have been performed only if the play had been produced in a different way. At first, for *La Cantatrice Chauve*, I had a more burlesque, more violent type of production in mind; somewhat in the style of the Marx Brothers, which would have created an explosive effect.

At the present time *La Cantatrice Chauve* does in fact end with the quarrel between the Smiths and the Martins. At this point the curtain is lowered and the play appears to begin again: the curtain is raised, the actors play the beginning of the first scene, then the final curtain falls.

I had imagined a more shattering ending. Two, even, whichever the actors preferred.

During the quarrel between the Smiths and the Martins the maid would make a fresh apparition and announce that dinner was served; all the action would cease, the two couples leaving the stage. As soon as it is empty, two or three accomplices in the audience start catcalling, kick up a row, shout protests and invade the stage. This brings on the manager of the theatre, followed by the Superintendent of Police and his men, who open fire at the rebellious audience (to make an example of them); then, while the manager and the superintendent congratulate each other on teaching the public a good lesson, the gendarmes, gun in hand, stand threateningly in front of the curtain and order the theatre to be cleared.

I was well aware that it was rather complicated to bring about an ending like this. It would have demanded a certain amount of courage and seven or eight additional actors for an extra three minutes. Too expensive. So I had written a

G

second ending, easier to put over . . . At the height of the Smith-Martin quarrel the maid arrives and announces the author in ringing tones.

The actors then respectfully make way, line up to the right and left of the stage and applaud the author, who comes quickly forward to face the public; then, shaking his fist at the audience, he cries: 'Load of skunks, I'll skin you alive!' The curtain would then fall very rapidly.

This ending was considered too polemical and not well enough related, anyway, to the stylised production and 'dignified' performances desired by the actors.

And it was because I did not find another ending that we decided not to finish the play at all, but to begin it again. To emphasize the interchangeability of the characters I had the simple idea of replacing the Smiths by the Martins in the repetition of the opening scene.

In Italy the producer has found another solution: the curtain falls on the quarrelling characters coming to blows in a kind of frenetic dance or balletic scrimmage. This is just as good.

(Published in the 'Cahiers des Saisons', 1959)

Les Chaises

TEXT FOR THE PROGRAMME OF THE *Théâtre du Nouveau Lancry*

At certain moments the world appears to me emptied of meaning, reality seems unreal. It is this feeling of unreality, the search for some essential reality, nameless and forgotten—and outside it I do not feel I exist—that I have tried to express through my characters, who drift incoherently, having nothing of their own apart from their anguish, their remorse, their failures, the vacuity of their lives. Human beings saturated in meaninglessness cannot be anything but grotesque, their sufferings cannot be anything but derisively tragic.

As the world is incomprehensible to me, I am waiting for someone to explain it . . .

(1952)

A LETTER TO THE FIRST PRODUCER

Cher Ami,

I realised after you left that we had taken the wrong turning; by this I mean that I have let you lead me into taking the wrong turning, so that we have not reached the heart of the play. I followed you and went astray with you, I lost sight of myself. No, you really haven't quite understood me in *Les Chaises:* and what is left to understand is precisely what is essential. Quite naturally you wanted to pull the play your way, when you should have given yourself up to it; a producer should let the play work on him. He should not want something from the play, he should efface himself, he should be the perfect receptacle. A conceited producer who wishes to impose 'his own personality' does not have a producer's vocation. Wheareas the author's job, on the contrary, demands of him that he should be conceited, impervious to others, and have an enlarged ego. If there is a crisis in the theatre, it is because there are vain producers who write the play themselves. It is not because *they* write the plays that there is a crisis in the theatre, but because all the time they are writing the *same* play, which is never the author's.

There is also the case of the producer who finds in a certain play seeds of talent that must be developed: intentions that must be made clearer and brought to light, or promising beginnings that must be realized. This may be the height of generosity on the producer's part . . . or simply vanity, if it means he considers he knows better than all the writers whose plays are shown to him.

This is not the case for you or me with regard to *Les Chaises*. Give yourself up to this play, I beg you. Do not minimise its effects, whether it be the large number of chairs, the large number of bells that announce the arrival of the invisible guests or the lamentations of the old woman, who should be like a weeping woman in Corsica or Jerusalem; everything should be exaggerated, excessive, painful, childish, a caricature, without finesse. It would be as serious a fault to mould the play as to mould the actors' interpretations. As for the latter, one only needs to press a button and start them moving: tell them all the time not to stop half-way but to follow right through and go all out. There must be plenty of great tragedy and biting irony. Allow yourself for a time to be moulded by the play.

On the other hand, when a certain passage shocks you and holds you up, when it seems to be 'not in its right place' or 'superfluous', do not yield whatever you do to your first impulse, which is to remove the obstacle; try rather to find a place for it, integrate it into the rhythm of the dramatic universe of the play, for this passage usually has its place, it has a meaning you have perhaps not yet realised, for you are perhaps still not quite in tune with the work, your rhythm is not the same as the poet's. Far more often than is thought, the cuts demanded by producers, as well as the passages they ask to be added, indicate a lack of understanding and go against the sense of the work, or rather express the clash of two wills or two visions, which cancel each other out. It is more in the nature of things for the producer to give way. And this submission reveals genuine pride; whereas his 'I know my job better than you do' is merely the expression of vanity and conflicts with the very vocation of a producer, whose authority is 'delegated', a function that suggests a more subtle and subordinate kind of pride.

It sometimes happens that an author fails to make himself clear. And yet he understands himself better than the producer and his instinct is almost always, if he is really a man of the theatre, more reliable. A genuine dramatist has the theatre in his bones, he expresses himself spontaneously in the medium of drama, which is his natural idiom.

The cuts you wanted me to make would remove the very passages whose purpose is, on the one hand, to express meaninglessness and arbitrariness, the vacuity of reality, language and human thought; and, on the other hand (above all), to let this vacuity slowly invade the stage, continually covering up, with words used like clothes, the absence of real people, the gaping holes in reality; for when the old couple speak they must never be allowed to forget 'the presence of this absence', which should be their constant point of reference, which they must constantly cultivate and sustain. Without it you could never suggest the unreal (for this can only be created by continual contrast with what is visible) and your production would be a failure, *Les Chaises* would no longer be *Les Chaises*. What is needed is plenty of gesture, almost pantomime, light, sound, moving objects, doors that open and close and open again, in order to create this emptiness, so that it grows and devours everything: absence can only be created in opposition to things present. And none of this would damage the movement, all these dynamic objects *are* the very movement of the play, though this may not as yet be movement as you see it.

Why can one see the Orator and not those other characters who crowd upon the stage? Does the Orator truly exist, is he real? Answer: he exists neither more nor less than the other characters. He is as invisible as the others, he is as real or as unreal, neither more nor less. Only one cannot do without his visible presence. He must be seen and heard because he is the last to remain on stage. But that he should be visible is a purely arbitrary convention, the only way of overcoming an otherwise insoluble technical problem.

One might as well assume, moreover, that the invisibility of the other characters is quite as much an arbitrary convention. All the characters could have been made visible if a striking enough method had been found of conveying theatrically their impalpable reality.

By the end of the play all this must create a 'shock'. The very last scene, after the disappearance of the old couple and the Orator's departure, must be very long: the sound of murmuring, of wind and water, should be heard for a very long time, as though coming from nothing, coming from the void. Thus the audience will not be tempted into giving the easiest explanation of the play, the wrong one. They must not be able to say, for example, that the old couple are mad or in their dotage and suffering from hallucinations; neither must they be able to say that the invisible characters are only the old couple's remorse and memories. This may perhaps be true up to a point, but it has absolutely no importance; the interest lies elsewhere. So there is one thing that can stop them interpreting the play in the usual dull way, psychologically or rationally: that these sounds, this intangible presence, should still be there for them, the audience, even after the departure of the three visible characters, and quite independent of the old couple's 'madness'. The tightly-packed crowd of non-existent beings should acquire an entirely objective existence of their own.

Contemporary drama is almost exclusively psychological, social, cerebral or . . . poetic. It is ametaphysical. *Les Chaises* is an attempt to push beyond the present frontiers of drama . . .

P.S. At one moment the old people should bring on the chairs without either of them speaking a word. This moment too should last a long time. One should give to their movements at this time a slightly balletic character (to the very discreet accompaniment of a waltz?)

(*Winter 1951-52*)

A LETTER TO A PRODUCER

January 1952
Cher ami . . .

Seeing that the theme of *Les Chaises* is the ontological 'void', or *absence*, I think the last decisive moment of the play should be the expression of this absence. So the curtain could perhaps fall long after the Orator, incapable (and with reason) of delivering his message, has come down from his platform, saluted the Emporor (a good theatrical moment to exploit) and gone out. At this moment the audience would have in front of them, bathed in a light that is once again dim and ghostly as at the beginning of the play (or equivalent to the lighting at the start of the play), empty chairs on an empty stage decorated with streamers, littered with useless confetti, which would give an impression of sadness, emptiness and disenchantment such as one finds in a ballroom after a dance; and it would be after this that the chairs, the scenery, the void, would inexplicably come to life (that is the effect, an effect beyond reason, true in its improbability, that we are looking for and that we must obtain), upsetting logic and raising fresh doubts. The lighting should grow pale and yellowish again, for it matches the action, and now the jamboree is over. This is anyway the ending I had in mind when I wrote the play, it was written *for* this ending, an ending I had envisaged before I started. I think we must go to extremes (if, by the way, you decide after all to use the blackboard, get the Orator to write this at the top: A A A A A A, nothing but A's).

I am, yours,

NOTES ON *Les Chaises*

23rd June 1951.

While I am writing *L'Orateur*[1], I can 'see' the 'invisible' characters very clearly. But just now I find it difficult to hear them talk. I suppose I must be tired.

[1] The first title of '*Les Chaises*'.

To express the void by means of language, gesture, acting and props.

To express absence.

To express regret and remorse.

The unreality of the real. Original chaos.

The voices at the end, the noises of the world, mutterings, the world in ruins, the world going up in smoke, in sounds and colours that fade away, the last foundations collapse or rather break up. Or melt into a sort of night. Or into a dazzling, blinding light.

The voices at the end: the sound of the world, of us, the audience.

Things can be said about this play which are contradictory and yet equally true.

On stage there is nothing; the two old people have hallu-cinations, the invisible characters are not there. Or again there really is nobody there at all, not even the two old people and the Orator, who are on the stage without being there: the old people and the Orator are not there any more than the invisible characters . . . They are as non-existent as the invisible ones or our dreams. Why, then, can one see *them* and not the others? But the play could have quite well been approached in a different way, with just a few of the guests appearing, without the Orator or the hosts. But why should one see anyone at all? This is obligatory, you have got to show something on a stage. But the two or three characters you do see in *Les Chaises* are in a way only what might be called the pivots of some mobile construction, largely invisible, evanescent, precarious, doomed to vanish like the world; for the characters themselves are unreal and yet the indispensable foundation of the whole structure. Or again it is all neither real nor unreal (what would that really mean?), but merely visible or invisible. And yet this nothing that is on the stage is the crowd. One must feel the presence of the crowd. So it is all the same whether you say there is nothing or a crowd of people on the stage.

One of my friends said to me: 'It's perfectly simple; what you mean is that the world is a subjective and arbitrary creation of our own minds?' Of *our own* minds, yes, not of *my* mind. I think I am inventing a new language, and I find that everyone speaks it already.

Or again the invisible characters: could they be an expression of reality imperfectly imagined, the product of an exhausted mind, no longer capable of imagining, inventing, and recreating the world, obsessed because it is feeble and defenceless, by absence and death?

The theatre may well be the only place where nothing ever really happens. A privileged place where nothing could ever happen.

To explain the end of *Les Chaises*: ' . . .The world is a desert. Peopled by phantoms with plaintive voices, it whispers love-songs over the gaping ruins of my emptiness! But gentle ghosts, return!' (Gérard de Nerval, *Promenades et Souvenirs*.) It could perhaps be that, without the gentleness.

ABOUT *JACQUES*

It is always difficult to say what one thinks about one's plays and about oneself. Whenever in the course of conversation I have managed to make some statement which has then been reproduced, I have either kicked myself for going too far or saying exactly the opposite of what I should have said.

Here, at any rate, are the plays: two burlesque comedies. One of them, *Jacques ou la Soumission*, was written in 1949 immediately after my first play, *La Cantatrice Chauve*, performed in 1950 at the '*Noctambules*'.

I believe *La Cantatrice Chauve* was one of the very first plays of what has been called the new post-war avant-garde theatre.

Like *La Cantatrice Chauve*, *Jacques* is a kind of parody or caricature of boulevard theatre, boulevard theatre going bad, gone mad. In *La Cantatrice Chauve* the characters spoke a language made of the most threadbare everyday clichés, so commonplace that banality acquired a certain strangeness. If I had not read Raymond Queneau's *Les Exercices de style*, I do not think I should ever have dared send *La Cantatrice Chauve* or anything else to a theatrical company.

A parody of family drama.

Jacques is primarily a family drama or a parody of family drama. It could be a moral play. Both the language and the behaviour of the characters are noble and distinguished. But this language gets dislocated and disintegrates. I wanted this 'naturalistic' comedy to be played so that I could somehow break away from it.

Le Tableau, the second play in the programme, could be a story of fairies and old witches, or an illustration of the miracles of medical science and plastic surgery[1] (the success of rejuvenation courses, skin grafting or the provision of missing members and organs, etc.), If there is anything else, the audience will notice it. Only broad comedy is good; I hope this is broad. And the comic is only comic if it is rather frightening. I wonder if mine is?

There is only one thing I am sure of, it is that my plays make no claim to save the world or prove that some men are better than others. As there is great precision and intelligence in Robert Postec's interpretation and production, dissatisfaction can only arise from the text itself.

(*L'Express*, October 1955)

[1]This sentence is a joke. Several critics have taken it as a basis for serious discussion.

ABOUT *COMMENT S'EN DÉBARRASSER*

There is no point in introducing a play in the theatre. It only needs to be presented. So I am not going to try and explain to you the play you are about to see and hear. A play cannot be explained, it must be acted; it is not a didactic demonstration, but a live show, a living witness.

All I can tell you is that this play is a simple work, childish and almost primitive in its simplicity. You will find no trace of symbolism in it. The story of this play could have been taken from a news item in any newspaper; it tells an ordinary story that could have happened to any one of us and must have happened to a great many of us. It is a slice of life, a realistic play.

If it can be criticised for being commonplace, it can certainly not be condemned for being untrue to life. So you will see mushrooms sprouting on the stage, which is incontrovertible proof not only that these mushrooms are *real* mushrooms, but that they are *normal* mushrooms too.

Of course some will say that everyone does not interpret reality as I do. There will certainly be people who think my vision of reality is in fact unreal or surrealist. I must say that personally I reject the kind of realism which is nothing but a sub-realism, using only two out of three or four or *n*-dimensions. This kind of realism alienates man from his profound self, which is his indispensable third dimension: without it man cannot begin to be his true self. What valuable truth can there be in a kind of realism that forgets to recognise the most profound human realities: the love, death, wonder, suffering and dreams that spring from our non-social self?

But it is not my intention to debate these problems in public. That is not my job. All I am trying to do is convince you that my attitude towards the characters you will soon see speaking and moving on the stage is completely objective. In fact I cannot prevent these images, objects, events and characters escaping from me. They do whatever they want, *they* control *me*, for it would be a mistake for *me* to try and control *them*. I am sure I should give them complete freedom, I can do nothing but obey their wishes. I do not like a writer who denies his characters freedom and turns them into spurious characters stuffed with ready-made ideas. If they do not suit his private political outlook, which does not stem from human truth but simply from some petrified ideology, he then twists them to his own purpose. But creation is not dictatorship, even *ideological* dictatorship. It is life and liberty, it can even stand against accepted ideals and turn against the author. An author has only one duty: not to intervene, to live and let live, to liberate his obsessions, his fantasies, his characters and his universe, to let them come alive, take shape and exist.

I hope the questions you might have put to me have been answered in advance. If you would like to know more, write to your dramatic critics, to Mr Harold Hobson and Mr Kenneth Tynan, it is their job to explain. I hope you have a pleasant evening.

(*Address delivered in French at the* Institut Français *in London, at a performance of* Comment s'en Débarrasser *by the French Company of Jean-Marie Serreau. December 1958.*)

RHINOCÉROS

For an American school edition with the French text
November 1960.

In 1938 the writer, Denis de Rougemont, was staying in Germany, at Nuremberg, during a Nazi demonstration. He tells us how he found himself in the midst of a dense crowd awaiting the arrival of Hitler. The people were beginning to show signs of impatience when the Führer and his entourage came in sight, at the far end of an avenue, looking very small in the distance. As they drew near the narrator watched the crowd, gradually caught up in a kind of hysteria, frenziedly acclaiming the sinister man. The hysteria spread and advanced, with Hitler, like a tide. This delirious enthusiasm first of all astonished the writer. But when the Führer came quite near and all the people round him gave way to the general hysteria, Denis de Rougemont felt the same raging madness in himself, struggling to possess him, a delirium that 'electrified' him. He was on the point of falling under the spell, when something rose from the depth of his being and resisted the rising storm. Denis de Rougemont tells us how uneasy he felt, how terribly alone in the crowd, offering hesitant resistance. His hair stood on end, 'literally' he says, and then he understood what is meant by Holy Terror. Just then it was not his mind that resisted, not arguments formulated in his brain, but his whole being, his whole 'personality' that bridled. There, perhaps, is the starting point of *Rhinocéros;* when one is assailed by arguments, theories, 'intellectual' slogans and all kinds of propaganda, it is probably impossible to give any explanation for this refusal. Later on, discursive reasoning will doubtless lend support to this natural instinctive resistance, this spiritual rejection. So Bérenger is not very sure at the time why he resists rhinoceritis, and this is proof that his resistance is genuine and profound. It may be that Bérenger is a man who, like Denis de Rougemont, is allergic to mass movements and marches of all kinds, military or not. *Rhinocéros* is certainly an anti-Nazi play, yet it is also and mainly an attack on collective hysteria and the epidemics that lurk beneath the surface of reason and ideas but are nonetheless serious collective diseases passed off as ideologies: once we realise that History has lost its reason, that lying propaganda masks a contradiction between the facts and the ideologies that explain them, once we cast a lucid eye on the world as it is to-day, this is enough to stop us being taken in by irrational 'reasons' and so help us not to lose our heads.

Indoctrinated champions of several different persuasions have obviously blamed the author for taking up an anti-intellectual attitude and choosing as principal hero a human being who is rather simple. But I considered it was not for me to present an emotional ideological system opposed to the other emotional ideological systems in force to-day. Quite simply I thought it was my job to reveal the inanity of these terrible systems, what they can lead to, how they stir people up, stupefy them and then reduce them to slavery. It will surely be apparent that the speeches of Botard, of Jean and Dudard are nothing but the pet shibboleths and slogans of various dogmas, concealing beneath a mask of cold objectivity the most irrational and violent pressures. *Rhinocéros* too is an attempt at 'demystification'.

At the request of the Optimates and Members of the College, we
reproduce the important Ionesco interviews himself, *a vital text*
from the point of view of theory, which successfully throws light on
alienation *and other Brechtianisms, and also on* non-participation
as recently upheld by M. Sartre.[1]

THE TRANSCENDANT SATRAP IONESCO INTERVIEWS HIMSELF[2]

EGO: My dear Alter-Ego, excuse me for waking you
              up so early, but will you interview me?

ALTER-EGO: *I wasn't asleep, don't apologise. I woke up,* cher
              Maître, *the same moment as you.*

EGO: Don't call me *cher Maître.* You know as well as
              I do how ridiculous I find these formal modes of
              address. Anyway I'm a long way from being a
              master. I'm not even a vice-master. Not even a
              half-master. A quarter-master, perhaps, and even
              then! . . .

ALTER-EGO: *You're very modest . . . What is all this about an*
              interview, anyway? . . .

EGO: '*France-Observateur*', in the person of one of its
              editors, kindly suggested I should introduce to
              its readers my play *Rhinocéros* and myself—before
              the First Night, which is about to take place at
              the *Odéon-Théâtre de France.* It's very important
              for me: and that's why I've come to ask you to
              ask me a few questions . . .

[1]Note from the Editor of the *Cahiers du Collège de Pataphysique.*
[2]'Satrapy' is the highest dignity conferred by the above College. According
to the members of the said College, Pataphysics is the science of sciences and
the ultimate philosophy. Alfred Jarry's character, Dr Faustroll, is its visible
and invisible spiritual Master. Pataphysicians, who are the disciples of Jarry
(the prophet of Faustroll), believe that we are all, consciously or not,
pataphysicians.

ALTER-EGO: *Why don't you get yourself interviewed by a professional journalist, by someone working for 'France-Observateur''? I'm hardly qualified to do it.*

EGO: Because it seems to me that talking to you I should be able to lead the discussion where I want. The questions you ask me will be easier so I can really shine in my answers and there'll be no risk of the questions being indiscreet. In a word they'll be questions I think I can forecast.

ALTER-EGO: *We don't know each other as well as you think. And if I was naughty, I could ask you some pretty embarrassing questions . . .*

EGO: That's just what I mean. Those are just the questions you're not to ask . . . I know the ones you mean! . . .

ALTER-EGO: *All right. Then just tell me the subject of your play.*

EGO: No! . . . That's not an interesting question. Besides, it's difficult to tell the story of a play. A play is a whole performance, the subject is only a pretext, and the text is only a score.

ALTER-EGO: *Well, tell us something about it, anyway! . . .*

EGO: All I can tell you is that *Rhinocéros* is the title of my play, *Rhinocéros*. And that my play, *Rhinocéros*, is about a lot of rhinoceroses; that 'unicornity' is a characteristic of some of them and 'bicornity' of others; but certain biological and psychical mutations can sometimes take place which completely upset . . .

ALTER-EGO (*yawning*): *You're going to bore everyone to death!*

EGO: Surely you don't imagine I'm going to amuse them! I'm writing didactic drama.

ALTER-EGO: *You astonish me. Weren't you quite recently the sworn enemy of that kind of drama?*

EGO: You can't write didactic drama when you're ignorant. I *was* ignorant, at least about some things, only a few months ago. So I set to work. Now I'm just like the Good Lord, the Devil, M. Sartre and Pico de la Mirandola, I know everything . . . but everything . . . And a lot of other things beside. In fact it's only when you know everything that you can be didactic. But it would be sheer pretention to try and be didactic when you don't know everything. And authors aren't like that!

ALTER-EGO: *You really know everything?*

EGO: Of course I do. For example, I know everything you can think. What do you know that I don't know!

ALTER-EGO: *And so you're writing didactic drama, anti-bourgeois drama?*

EGO: That's it. Bourgeois drama is magic drama, spellbinding, drama that asks the audience to identify itself with the heroes of the play, drama of participation. Anti-bourgeois drama is a drama of non-participation. A bourgeois public falls into the trap. A non-bourgeois public, a people's audience, has a different mentality: it puts a certain distance between itself and the heroes of the play on the stage. It alienates itself from the theatrical illusion in order to watch the play with a clear mind and pass judgment on it.

ALTER-EGO: *Give me some examples.*

EGO: Here you are: just now, at the '*Ambigu*', they're playing *Madame Sans-Gêne* to packed houses. It's a public of bourgeois intellectuals, a public that 'participates'.

ALTER-EGO: *What do you mean?*

EGO: The theatregoers identify themselves with the heroes of the play. You can hear remarks like this in the audience: 'Let him have it, Charlie!', 'Serves him right!', 'You've had it!', and so on. A peoples' audience is clear-headed and could never be so simple-minded. Besides, up to the present day, all our drama has always been written by and for the middle-classes, who have deliberately kept the clear-headed people's audience away. Like me, you must have read *Le Petit Chose* by Alphonse Daudet. You remember how, when Le Petit Chose had become an actor, he joined a company that went round the suburbs playing melodramas on an improvised stage. Daudet tells us that Le Petit Chose, who always played the scheming villain, had to leave by a secret door, because the public was waiting for him after the performance to lynch him in front of the theatre: that's just another example of the stupidity of the 'participation' of bourgeois intellectuals. The good people of Shakespeare's time 'participated' too: they laughed and cried at the show, in a thoroughly middle-class way. In the Middle Ages too, in the forecourts of the cathedrals, the audience was purely middle-class, because they identified themselves, because they 'took part'. The famous theory of 'catharsis' also assumes some identification with the action and the tragic characters, otherwise no-one could have been purged; but we all know that all the Greeks were exclusively middle-class. You know the negro spirituals. They're spellbinding. A dangerous sense of communion is established between the singers and the public . . .

ALTER-EGO: *And that means what?*

EGO: It proves that all blacks are bourgeois . . . Primitive peoples have various kinds of entertainment, half magic, half religious rites, which again rely on participation; but we all know that savages are bourgeois intellectuals too. Egyptian drama is also drama of participation. And, of course, everything prehistorical was bourgeois!

ALTER-EGO: *I think it's rather risky to claim that the middle-classes go so far back in time . . . they're the product of the French Revolution, of our industrial civilisation, of capitalism. Any schoolboy can tell you that. Could you maintain, for example, that . . .*

EGO: I maintain that Abraham himself was a bourgeois. Didn't he rear sheep? He must certainly have had some textile factories.

ALTER-EGO: *The Swine!*

EGO: To return to my rhinoceroses, after this historical survey for which I apologise . . .

ALTER-EGO: *It was most instructive . . .*

EGO: . . . I feel I must point out that I've been quite masterly in my avoidance of drama of participation. In fact the heroes of my play, all except one, transform themselves in front of the public's very eyes (for this is a realistic piece) into wild beasts, into rhinoceroses. I hope my audiences will be disgusted with them, Disgust alienates more completely than anything else. And so I shall have achieved the "distanciation" of the public from the performance. Disgust is lucidity.

ALTER-EGO: *You say that in your play only one of the characters is not transformed.*

EGO: Yes, he doesn't catch rhinoceritis.

ALTER-EGO: *Does this still mean that the audience shouldn't identify themselves with the hero who remains human?*

EGO: On the contrary, they should identify themselves with him absolutely.

ALTER-EGO: *Then you yourself are still committing the sin of identification.*

EGO: That's true . . . But as the play also has the virtue of non-participation or alienation, we can claim this play has realised a synthesis of drama that is both bourgeois and anti-bourgeois, thanks to an instinctive skill which is my own . . .

ALTER-EGO: *You're talking rubbish, old man.*

EGO: I know! But I'm not the only one.

(*In* 'Cahiers du Collège de Pataphysique', *March* 1960; *first published in* 'France-Observateur' *in January* 1960.)

RHINOCÉROS

In the course of my life I remember being very much struck by what one might call current opinion: it develops so rapidly and is so contagious that it soon grows into a regular epidemic.

Suddenly people get caught up in some new religion or fanatical doctrine; in short, in what professors of philosoply and the ragged philosophers of journalism call "the inevitable historical moment". Then what takes place is really a mental mutation. I don't know whether you have noticed, but when people no longer share your opinion, when you can no longer reach an understanding with them, you have the impression you are trying to get through to monsters . . .

To rhinoceroses?

For example. They have the same mixture of ingenuousness and ferocity. They would kill you without a qualm if you did not think as they do. And in the last quarter of this century history has given us clear proof that people transformed in this way are not just *like*, but truly *become* rhinoceroses. Now it is quite possible, although it may seem extraordinary, for there to be a few individual consciences that stand for the Truth *against* History, or against what is called History. There is a myth about History, and it is high time it was "demythified" to recall a fashionable expression. There have always been a few isolated consciences to stand against the rest of the world and represent the universal conscience. Even revolutionaries are so isolated at the start that they have a bad conscience and are not sure whether they are right or wrong. I just cannot understand how they have ever found the courage to continue quite alone. They are heroes. As soon as the truth for which they give their lives is officially accepted, there are no more heroes, only bureaucrats, craven and cautious as befits their function. That is the whole theme of *Rhinocéros*.

Tell us something about its form.

What do you want me to tell you about it? This play is perhaps a little longer than the others. But just as traditional

and as classical in conception. I respect the fundamental laws
of the theatre: a simple idea, an equally simple development
and a neat ending.

> (Remarks collected by Claude Sarraute.
> *Le Monde*, the 19th of January 1960)

A NOTE ON *Rhinocéros*

In a recent number of "*Arts*" my critic, and friend notwithstanding, Pierre Marcabru, considers this play to be the "reactionary" expression of an outsider's refusal to join in the
human adventure. I must say that the play really was meant
to show the Nazification of a country as well as the confusion
of a man who, naturally immune to the disease, witnesses
the mental metamorphosis of the community in which he
lives. Originally "rhinoceritis" was indeed a form of Nazism.
Between the two world wars, Nazism was largely invented
by the fashionable intellectuals, ideologists and pseudo-intel-
lectuals who spread the doctrine. They were rhinoceroses.
Even more than the mob they have the mentality of the mob.
They do not think, they recite "intellectual" slogans.

Rhinocéros, which is now being acted in a number of countries, makes a surprisingly strong impression on audiences of
every kind. Is it because this play is a vague attack on all sorts
of things? This is one reproach levelled at me, though others
specially blame me for only attacking Nazi totalitarianism.
And is it really refusing the human adventure to stand up to the
collective hysteria, even if backed by philosophy, to which
whole nations periodically fall victim? Is it not in fact astonishing that the vicissitudes of such a lonely and individualistic
character as the hero of my play should appeal to so many

people throughout the world? And is it not in our profound isolation, far beyond sophistry and schism, that this universal fraternity finds common ground? In spite of the well-reasoned objections of so many distinguished critics people have responded sympathetically to my chief character, which would rather seem to prove that it is not this odd man out who is cut off from the human adventure, but our harebrained ideologists instead. I wonder if I have hit upon a new plague of modern times, a strange disease that thrives in different forms but is in principle the same. Automatic systematised thinking, the idolisation of ideologies, screens the mind from reality, perverts our understanding and makes us blind. Ideologies too raise the barricades, dehumanise men and make it impossible for them to be *friends notwithstanding;* they get in the way of what we call co-existence, for a rhinoceros can only come to terms with one of his own kind, a sectarian with a member of his particular sect.

I believe Jean-Louis Barrault has caught the meaning of the play and put it over perfectly. The Germans turned it into tragedy, Jean-Louis Barrault into terrible farce and fantastic fable. Both interpretations are valid, exemplary productions of this play.

(*Arts* January 1961)

ABOUT *Rhinocéros* IN THE UNITED STATES

I am delighted that *Rhinocéros* is a popular success in New York, but at the same time surprised and saddened. I was present at only one almost complete rehearsal before the first night. I must admit I was completely baffled. As far as I could see they had turned Bérenger's friend, Jean, a character that is hard, fierce and disturbing into a comic figure, a *feeble* rhinoceros. It also seemed to me that the production had turned Bérenger himself, an irresolute character, a reluctant hero, allergic to this epidemic of rhinoceritis, into a kind of tough hard-headed intellectual, a kind of unruly revolutionary who knows quite well what he is doing (and though he knows, does not wish to explain the reasons for his attitude). I also saw on the stage some boxing-bouts that do not figure in the text, intro-duced by the producer. I wonder why? I have often been at odds with my producers: either they are not daring enough and reduce the impact of my plays by not exhausting their full potentialities as the stage demands: or else they 'adorn' the text, overloading it with cheap embellishment and decoration, un-necessary and therefore worthless. I am not writing literature. I am doing something quite different: I am writing drama. I mean that my text is not just dialogue, but also 'stage directions'. These should be respected as much as the text, they are essen-tial, they are also sufficient. If I gave no indication that Bérenger and Jean should come to blows on the stage and pull each other's noses, it is because I had no desire for them to do so.

I have read the American critics on the play and noticed that everyone agreed the play was funny. Well, it isn't. Although it is a farce, it is above all a tragedy. The production reveals not only an absence of style (as in everything put on in the boule-vard theatres of Paris or on Broadway; and in Moscow too, moreover, where the advanced theatre is the old theatre of 1900) but above all intellectual dishonesty. We actually wit-ness a mental transformation in a whole group of people; the old values are degraded and overthrown, new ones emerge and triumph. One man helplessly sees his whole world transformed and can do nothing to stop it: he no longer knows if he is right or wrong; he struggles but without hope; he is the last of his species. He is lost. This is thought to be funny. The New York critics agreed unanimously. Barrault, on the other hand, has made a tragic farce of it: a farce, yes, but an oppressive one. Moretti, the Italian actor who has just died and was one of the greatest actors in the world, made a sad and moving drama of it. Stroux, the producer in Düsseldorf, and his leading actor, Karl Maria Schley, turned it into a stark tragedy with no concessions, barely relieved by its cold irony; the Poles made it a weighty play. But Mr. Antoni, acting on the advice of Heaven-knows-who, and certainly not the author, has made it into something funny and 'anti-conformist'. Now there is something too imprecise about conformism. Strictly speaking, my play is not even a satire: it is a fairly objective description of the growth of fanaticism, of the birth of a totalitarianism that grows, propagates, conquers, transforms a whole world and, naturally, being totalitarian transforms it totally. The play should trace and point the different stages of this phenomenon. I really tried to say this to the American producer; I clearly indicated in the few interviews I was able to give that the aim of this play was to denounce, to expose, to show how an ideology gets transformed into idolatry, how it seeps into everything, how it reduces the masses to hysteria, how an idea, which was reasonable enough for discussion at the start, can become monstrous when leaders, then totalitarian dictators, governing islands, acres or continents, use it as a powerful stimulant, a strong dose of which has a malignant and monstrous effect on the "people", turning them into an hysterical mob. I had made it quite clear that I was not attacking conformism, for there is a certain anti-conformism which is conformist in so far as the conformism it attacks is merely something vague. An anti-conformist play may be amusing; an anti-totalitarian play, for example, is not. It cannot be anything else but painful and serious.

Some critics blame me for denouncing evil without saying what good is. I have been reproached for not letting Bérenger say what ideology inspired his resistance. They take this to be a fundamental objection: but it is so easy to rely on a system of thought that is more or less mechanical. If I asked Mr Walter Kerr, the dramatic critic of the *New York Herald Tribune*, to define his personal philosophy for me, he would be highly embarrassed. And yet it is for him and not for me to find the answer, for him and the other critics, and above all for the audience. Personally I mistrust the intellectuals who for thirty-odd years have done nothing but propagate different forms of rhinoceritis and who merely provide a philosophical justification for those waves of collective hysteria that periodically sweep over whole nations. Is it not the intellectuals who are the inventors of Nazism? If I set up a ready-made ideology in opposition to other ready-made ideologies, which clutter up the brain, I should only be opposing one system of rhinoceric slogans to another. There was once a time when, if someone uttered the word "Jew" or "Bolshevist", people would lower their horns and charge off to kill a Jew or a Bolshevist and anyone accused of compromise with a Jew or a Bolshevist. Nowadays if someone utters the word "bourgeois" or in any part of the wide world "capitalist Imperialist", everyone charges off just as stupidly, just as blindly, to kill the bourgeois or the capitalist without having the slightest idea what lies behind the insult or why it has been used, without even knowing what kind of person tries to incite others to do his own dirty work or what private motives provoke such monstrous violence. It seems to me absurd to ask a dramatist to produce a bible, a way to salvation, it is absurd to think for a whole world and give it some automatic philosophy: a playwright poses problems. People should think about them, when they are quiet and alone, and try and resolve them for themselves, without constraint; an unworkable solution one has found for oneself is infinitely more valuable than a ready-made ideology that stops men from thinking.

Besides, personally, I have my own answer: if I gave it away it would lose its force; like a key, it would have no further use and become a pass-key, another system of slogans leading to a new form of rhinoceritis.

One of the great critics in New York complains that, after destroying one conformism, I put nothing else in its place, leaving him and the audience in a vacuum. That is exactly what I wanted to do. A free man should pull himself out of vacuity on his own, by his own efforts and not by the efforts of other people.[1]

(*Arts*, 1961)

[1] *Rhinocéros* has to date had more than a thousand performances in Germany, hundreds in the Americas and in France. Many others in England, Italy, Poland, Japan, Scandinavia, Czekoslovakia, Yugoslavia, Holland etc. . . etc. . . I am amazed at the success of this play. Do people understand it properly? Do they see in it that monstrous phenomenon of 'massification'? And while they are all 'massifiable', are they also, essentially and in their heart of hearts, all individualists, unique human beings?

4. TO TRY TO BELONG TO ONE'S OWN TIME IS ALREADY TO BE OUT OF DATE

NOTES ON THE THEATRE

I sometimes feel in this world of ours as if I was at a show; though these are, needless to say, rare moments of tranquillity. Everything around me is a show. An incomprehensible show. A show made up of forms, moving shapes, lines of force that conflict and annihilate one another, ravelling and unravelling themselves. What an extraordinary machine! Not tragic, but stupefying. Wonder is my basic emotional reaction to the world. Not tragic — all right; then comic perhaps, strangely comic indeed, derisory, this world of ours. And yet if I take a closer look at it, a kind of searing pain takes hold of me. This pain in itself astonishes me; this searing feeling itself is steeped in strangeness. I am infinitely surprised that things exist, and events and passions, and the colours and cares of both night and day, ephemeral though, transparent and intangible: the fruits of chaos. And all these shifting shapes conflict and collide in mutual destruction.

I turn my gaze outwards, I look into myself and I murmur: this is not possible, this is too improbable, it is not true and it cannot last. It will indeed not last. It is as though I were witnessing the disintegration of this complex pattern of shapes and movement, this semblance of things and beings. I have the impression that by writing plays I am helping to accelerate this process of disintegration. For all this has become a painful obsession to me. I should like, for once, to get rid of this dream-like world, of this dream of a world, which in the end so dulls my sense of wonder that it fades into a habit and I reach a state of boredom, disquiet, and depression.

Sometimes I manage to love existence and the world. I discover beauty in it. I believe I have discovered 'Beauty' there and I become attached to it.

I participate, if not in this or that particular passion, at least in the general dynamism of existence, I am caught up in the movement, I let myself drift, it is as though I was rapt in this unaccustomed and attractive universe, surrounded by the halo of creation. The misty spectacle of the incomprehensible surrounds me on every side.

. . . Quite honestly, I like all this less and less, it wearies me more and more. I sometimes feel a real need to touch something solid; when someone knocks against me or hurts me, it seems to me that there really *is* something there. And yet I know there is nothing but evanescence, everything moving towards dissolution; I am dying myself and nothing remains of nothing. Other fruits of chaos will appear again, other flowers from the void, other vaporous worlds, movements, shapes and colours, without reason, with no foundation.

Nothing is atrocious, everything is atrocious. Nothing is comic. Everything is tragic. Nothing is tragic, everything is comic, everything is real, unreal, possible, impossible, conceivable, inconceivable. Everything is heavy, everything is light . . .

I have been called a writer of the absurd; this is one of those terms that go the rounds periodically, it is a term that is in fashion at the moment and will soon be out of fashion. It is vague enough now, in any case, to mean nothing any more and to be an easy definition of anything. If when a little time has passed I have not been forgotten, there will be another vogue word on everybody's lips, another accepted term with which to define me and others without defining us.

In reality, the existence of the world seems to me not absurd but unbelievable, yet intrinsically, within the framework of existence and the world, one can see things clearly, discover laws and establish "rational" rules. The incomprehensible appears to us only when we return to the very springs of existence; when we take up a position in the sidelines and obtain a total picture of it.

NOTES ON THE THEATRE 1953

Pure drama, or shall we say tragic action, is then the following: an action of universal significance, serving as a pattern or prototype, which embraces and reflects all the particular stories and actions that belong to the same category as the model action represented. (Universality or permanence is rejected in our own Heraclitic-Hegelian-Marxist period. I am, however, convinced that in reaction to our own period, as is customary, a later period governed by a new intellectual fashion will one of these days rehabilitate universal ideas.)

As for me, sometime I should like to be able to strip dramatic action of all that is particular to it: the plot, the accidental characteristics of the characters, their names, their social setting and historical background, the apparent reasons for the dramatic conflict, and all the justifications, explanations and logic of the conflict. This conflict would have to exist, or else there would be no drama, but no-one would know the reason for it. One may speak of the dramatic quality of a painting, or representational works like those of Van Gogh, or of non-representational works. This dramatic quality quite simply springs from a clashing of forms and lines, from abstract antagonisms, without psychological motivation. One speaks of the dramatic quality of a musical work. One can also say that a natural phenomenon (storms) or a landscape is dramatic. The importance and the truth of this "dramatisation" reside in the fact that it cannot be explained. In the theatre one looks for a motive. And in the theatre of to-day it is being increasingly looked for. In this way the theatre is being devalued.

With spoken choruses and a central mime as soloist (perhaps assisted by two or three others at the most), one could by means of set gestures, a few words and pure movement succeed in expressing pure conflict, pure drama in its essential truth, and reproduce the permanently destructive and self-destructive pattern of existence itself: pure reality, non-logical and non-psychological (transcending what to-day is called absurd and non-absurd), impellent and expellent forces.

But how does one manage to represent the non-representable? How do you represent the non-representational and *not* represent the representational?

It is all very difficult. Let us try at least to "particularise" as little as possible, to dematerialise as much as we can, or else do something different: invent a unique event, unlike and unconnected with any other event; create an inimitable universe, foreign to all the others, a new cosmos within the cosmos with its own laws and consistencies, an idiom that could belong to nothing else: a world that could be nothing but *my own*, irresolvable but still in the end able to be communicated, substituted for that other world with which other people could identify themselves (I fear none of this is really possible).

It is, however, true that self in the absolute is the universal.

Above all make no effort to achieve what is called the "popular" theatre. Drama "for the people" should be rejected for the same reasons as so-called "bourgeois" or "boulevard" drama.

Why? Because "popular" theatre as well as "bourgeois' theatre is "non-popular" theatre. Both are equally cut off from the profound springs of the human soul. Both are the products of people who live confined in their own little world, prisoners of their ideological obsessions, which express nothing but their own schizophrenia, although they mistake them for fundamental truths that must irrevocably be passed on to the whole world. In reality, their "popular" theatre is a theatre of edification and political instruction.

Boulevard theatre, which is accused of being bourgeois, that is to say of belonging to a minority, is however, curiously enough, accepted quite spontaneously by the great public drawn from every class.

A boulevard play pleases a banker, a civil servant, a little clerk, my own concierge, and a working man, etc.

I am in favour of anti-theatre in so far as it could be an anti-bourgeois and anti-popular theatre (assuming one understands by anti-popular theatre this didactic drama we have just mentioned). Deliberately to try and popularise the theatre is in the long run to vulgarise it, to simplify it and turn it into something rudimentary. Bourgeois drama too is vulgar and facile drama ... because it is "popular".

But drama that really came from the "people", by that I mean from the supra-social depths of the mind, would in the present state of affairs be accepted neither by the bourgeois or the socialists, nor by the intellectuals who swarm through the newspaper offices and the cafés of Saint-Germain-des-Prés.

What we need is mythical drama: *that* would be universal. The drama of ideas is also, in spite of itself, a drama of myths ... but degraded ones: ideas that are not equivalent to an Idea.

A drama that really sprang from the soul of the people would be primitive and rich; pseudo-popular, didactic drama is merely primary, elementary. I am all for primitive drama, and against primary drama.

Of course everyone cannot succeed in writing for everyone. It is no simple matter to reach those springs of the mind that are common and universal. One must write for oneself, for it is in this way that one may reach others.

FURTHER NOTES

It has rightly been said that the theatre is lagging behind other manifestations of art and literature in our own time; modern art and literature are what they are because they have been treading a narrow path, because they have been made by specialists for specialists or for particularly enlightened enthusiasts; there is a world of letters just as there is a world of philatelists, of numismatists, of mathematicians etc. . . . Albert Thibaudet was right to say that the circle of literature is as restricted as the circle of mathematics. No more than the other arts can the theatre (especially as it is lagging behind) turn back in its tracks. The direction in which it must evolve *cannot* be other (if it is not to enter a period of degradation) than along the narrow path followed by contemporary poetry, painting and music. Béla Bartok and Schoenberg did not write music for the Place Pigalle, music appreciated by the *midinettes;* they left this task to the Charles Trenets; neither at the moment are Picasso and the abstract painters appreciated by business men, *midinettes*, tradesmen or *petit bourgeois*, whether they be communist or anti-communist; nor by coarse-grained double-dealers and stupid sergeant-majors and dictators; Henri Michaux cannot write poems to be set to music by singers like Trenet etc. None of these people are to be despised. Of course they're not. It is just that there is a problem of initiation in philosophy, mathematics, music, the plastic arts and literature, etc.

The existence of different mentalities raises no insurmountable barriers, there are no real divisions: bourgeois drama is more popular than the "popular" drama fabricated by intellectuals or semi-intellectuals. A football match can number among its fans the milkman, the factory-hand and the minister of finance. Here the initiation is easy. But there is not one class of football fans. Neither is there one "class" of bourgeois followers of bourgeois art. Simply people who are initiated, who have the possibility of appreciating what any normal, reasonably cultured mind could appreciate at some level or other.

Drama ought to be divided into different categories, entirely distinct, and classified by the Minister of Fine Arts or by the Prefect of Police for different kinds of public, with posters at the entrance indicating categories A, B, C, D etc.

My objection to the Brechtians is that they are terrorists.

I believe that several kinds of theatre can co-exist and that the stylistic unity of a period is the resultant of all its contradictions and variety.

We can and should have theatres seating two thousand or even forty thousand for the unenlightened. This would be a theatre of patronage, ranging from Brecht to the Boy Scouts. Or something different: arenas for competitions between horses, dogs, bulls or gladiators, which would satisfy the head of the state, the scientist and the ignorant man at one and the same time.

We could also have theatres of five hundred to a thousand seats for a public initiated to the theatre without being fully

230 Notes and Counter-notes

initiated, able to like Shakespeare, Molière and Ibsen, but not particularly interested in "experiments".

And finally we could have theatres seating from fifty to a hundred people, which would be designed for the specialists or semi-specialists in artistic experiments.

The tragic: when the whole destiny of man is summarised in one model situation (with or without divine transcendence).

The dramatic: a particular case, particular circumstances and a particular destiny.

The tragic: destiny in a general or collective sense; a revelation of "the human condition".

I myself participate in a drama: I see reflected there *my own* case (the painful things that happen on the stage can happen to me).

Tragedy: what happens on the stage can happen to *us*. It can concern *us all* (and no longer just *myself*).

The theatre can be the place where something really seems to be happening.

The presence of other people had become unbearable to me. It was horrible to listen to them, painful to speak to them, terrible to have anything to do with them or feel them around me. It made me quite ill to watch them toiling away, rushing about, swooping here and there, or amusing themselves mindlessly, playing bowls or *belote*. And their machines, their machines! Great trucks, motor cycles, motors of every kind, electric appliances, lifts and vacuum cleaners all mixed up with their aspirations and their expirations. It was the limit, really the limit: strangeness with a vengeance.

The world ought not to interest me so much. In reality, I am obsessed with it. Those who proclaim themselves the friends of man are in reality indifferent and detached: they love mankind only in the abstract.

Ah! If only men were asses or oxen, they would no longer get on my nerves! I should like to be the only man surrounded by a horde of asses and oxen. Ah! If only that were possible!

Look at the young. They are exactly the same as the young people when I was young. They all amuse themselves in the same way, exactly as they have always done, century after century: the same rowdyism, the same bright remarks, the same insolence, the same fatuity and the same folly, which will be succeeded as it has been throughout the centuries by the same wisdom in the mature adult. One fine day they will grow old in the same way, with the same feeling of revolt or resignation, or the same incomprehension as all those other young people who have grown old in preceding generations. The same mannerisms, the same violence: I have never liked the young or the old.

The world does not seem a prototype any more, it is stereotyped and standardised. The strange becomes boring or terrifying: it can no longer be anything but realistic, a realistic nightmare.

THEATRE FROM WITHIN

A programme note for a revival of Victimes du devoir *at the Théâtre de Babylone* (1954).

I am neither prosecuting nor defending, but I believe that drama orientated towards some goal outside itself can appeal only to the most superficial part of human beings. I believe that the social crust and discursive thought conceal man from himself and cut him off from his most deeply repressed desires, his most essential needs, his myths, his indisputable anguish, his most secret reality and his dreams. All drama tied to a cause,

H*

whatever this may be, withers away as soon as the ideology it serves is seen to be worthless.

The obligations and restrictions of the outside world can never stop me finding myself alone, some morning in June grappling with creation in renewed consciousness of the wonder of being.

I am waiting for beauty to come, one day, and illuminate or shine through the sordid walls of my everyday prison. The chains that bind me are ugliness, sadness, poverty, old age and death. What revolution could deliver me from these?

Only when I am no longer troubled by the mystery of my own existence shall I have some leisure left over to settle accounts with those who accompany me on my journey.

FRAGMENT FROM A LETTER 1957

It is seven years since my first play was acted in Paris. It was a tiny failure, a minor scandal. The failure of my second play was already a bit more resounding, and the scandal a little more serious. It was with *Les Chaises* in 1952 that things really began to happen: eight disgruntled people were in the audience every night, but rumours about the play were already beginning to reach a much greater number of people in Paris and as far as the German frontier. With my third, fourth, fifth, and so on up to my eighth play, each flop became more and more gigantic: protestations floated across the Channel, over the Pyrenees and into Germany, passed the frontiers of Spain and Italy and took the boat for England. Can quantity turn into quality? I think it can, since the ten flops have now proved successful.

If I go on having failures like this, I shall soon have achieved a positive triumph.

ANOTHER FRAGMENT

I already have quite a large number of plays behind me, written and acted: a whole world, several different worlds and characters. I should like to produce more. It is my greatest delight, perhaps the only one. I have taken to 'writing'. How curious. Half pleasure, half chore. Writing, producing plays, is not an escape: but the joy of creation. For the moment mine is a fresh world. It is alive. When the time comes, of course, it will no longer mean a thing. Either it will be too hackneyed or it will have withered away like a dead leaf. It is so fragile; it is evanescent. But the Universe of the Good Lord Himself is fragile and evanescent. This does not stop the Good Lord from creating Universes destined to disappear, or rather to be overlaid. If *He* creates such worlds — I still have a reason to create some for myself! I do not know, and yet I tell myself I am beginning to believe that to have created these works — is to have done my duty. I do not know why, but I am beginning to tell myself this. Whether my plays have great value or not is of little consequence. They are what they are, but they *are*.

FURTHER NOTES 1960

As soon as one starts admitting that a work of art, an event or a political or economic system can be two or three things at once, that (and this is the case) several interpretations can exist together, which all more or less account for the facts in a manner satisfactory to our understanding; when Hegel and Spengler and Marx and Toynbee and René Guénon and theology and psycho-analysis and Lupasco all seem to give a valid explanation of history that satisfies me objectively; when every ideology loses its persuasive and compulsive force; when belief in an ideology is merely a matter of choice, when this choice may well be irrational and even a rational choice can be made in error, then all our thoughts and all our ideologies cancel out.

And then what? What is there that can offer us a 'true' image of the universe? Well, there is art and science.

Very few people 'think': very few per nation. And even then, as these men have no access to the most closely-guarded secrets of science and research any more than politics, not to speak of the best-kept secrets of the police and those who secretly control our propanganda, these thinkers cannot be more than journalists or marionettes. Words of command are rapped out, thought up in hidden places, where a few initiates have discussed the matter: co-existence, the inevitability of conflict or the reverse, peace, aggression, imperialism or non-imperialism. Immediately the 'thinkers' seize on these words, get excited and ideologise. And whole — more or less primitive — tribes of intellectuals and artists take these few thinkers on trust, repeat their sayings, follow them and abstain from questioning. Whereas the former were marionettes, the latter are parrots.

In short, one can subscribe to *any* ideology, as it can never be proved wrong by facts. Yet it can never be really proved right either. It is always open to argument. An ideology is a system of estimates or hypotheses, verifiable or not according to whether one is passionately, hence obscurely and with one's whole being, *for* or *against* that particular ideology. The scientist is obliged to seek, to research, to experiment and to submit to objective verification. His work may be invalidated or confirmed by the facts. He must constantly re-examine (himself). He is forced to be objective.

But an ideologue is not bound by any precise or effective discipline, he can say what he likes, he can claim and justify everything and prove to us that everything enters into his system. Everything does indeed seem to enter into *every* system.

I am not an ideologue, for I am straightforward and objective. I am an artist, a creator of characters: my characters cannot lie, they can only be what they are. They would be only too pleased to lie, but they really find it impossible: for if they lied, everyone would notice, since they would have to lie in full view of the public. Art does not lie, art is true. (Even a lie is revealing, in art. In an ideologist, it masks his own complexes.)

A work of art is not a reflection, *an image* of the world; but it is made *in the image of the world*.

I have always been obsessed by death. Since the age of four, when I first knew I was going to die, this anguish has never left me. It was as though I had suddenly realised that there was no way of escape and nothing to be done about it.

Moreover, I have always been aware of the impossibility of communication, of isolation and encirclement; I write in order to fight encirclement; I also write in order to cry out my fear of death and my humiliation at the thought of dying. To live in order to die is not *absurd*, it is just the way things are. Agonising thoughts like these cannot be stigmatised as bourgeois or anti-bourgeois, they lie too deep for that.

The things my characters say are usually very dull, because banality is a symptom of non-communication. Men hide behind their clichés.

Robert Kanters has remarked that there are two kinds of dramatic language in my plays: 'simple expressions or ready-made phrases, and something quite extraordinary that verges on the fantastic or even belongs entirely to fantasy'.

It is indeed a characteristic of madness when the truth is masked by language which, although authentic, is meaningless and therefore unrevealing. It is as if there were some fundamental reality that can be expressed only in everyday conversation, which either co-exists with the text or disrupts it.

I was astonished to see there was a great resemblance between Feydeau and myself . . . not in the themes or subjects of the plays, but in the rhythm and their structure. The development of a play like *La Puce à l'oreille*, for example, demands a pace that rapidly quickens to a dizzy climax, the movement lies in a kind of lunatic progression; there I seem to recognise my own obsession with proliferation. Perhaps that is the source of comedy, this wild and disorderly progression in the movement of a play. There is a progression in tragedy or drama too, a kind of accumulation of effects. In a drama the acceleration is not so fast, it is more carefully controlled and there is a better braking system. In a comedy the movement seems to have got out of control. The author no longer drives the machine, the machine is driving him. There perhaps lies the difference between the comic and the tragic.

Take a tragedy, accelerate the movement, and you will have a comic play: empty the characters of all their psychological content, and again you will have a comic play; make of your characters people who are purely social, caught up in the social machine, for their social 'truth', and again you will have a play that is comic . . . or tragi-comic.

RECENT NOTES

Certain critics accuse me of defending an *abstract* humanism, a man who exists nowhere. In reality I am in favour of man wherever he exists: of my enemy as well as my friend. Man everywhere is concrete man. Abstract man is ideological man: and it is ideological man who does not exist. The essential condition of man is not man as a citizen but man as a mortal. When I speak about death, everyone understands me. Death is neither bourgeois nor socialist. It is my deepest anguish, all that comes from the deepest part of myself, which is the most 'popular', as it speaks to all the people.

Bernard Dort in his book on Brecht remarks that Brechtian theories have also spread to the cinema. This Brechtianism is, he says, an epidemic, but a healthy one. This delirious young critic talks exactly like my character Dudard who, speaking of rhinoceritis, declared that there are some diseases that are good for you.

Universal degeneration is confounded by scientific or artistic creation, even if the latter does show us a picture of decadence or stagnation in all its reality: to become aware of it is already to transcend it.

Knowledge and creation, imitation and invention, the real and the imaginary meet and mingle.

We carry a potential work of art within us, long before it sees the light of day.

It merely waits for the chance to emerge.

Another kind of drama is still possible. More powerful and far richer. Drama that is not symbolist, but symbolic; not allegorical, but mythical; that springs from our everlasting anguish; drama where the invisible become visible, where ideas are translated into concrete images, of reality, where the problem is expressed in flesh and blood; where anguish is a living presence, an impressive witness; drama that might puzzle the sociologists but could stimulate and quicken all that is unscientific in the scientist; and, reaching beyond his ignorance, the common man.

However, I must confess I seem to notice something rather

strange happening nowadays to works of literature and drama. I really have the impression that critical discussion is rarely centred on the works themselves; it is usually off the target. It is as if a work is of interest only if it offers a good pretext for discussion. So first of all a dramatist is asked to explain his own plays: and his explanations seem to arouse more enthusiasm than the works themselves, which are what they *are* and should explain themselves. It is rather up to those who see or read a play to explain it, beginning and ending with the play itself, and they should avoid all the commentaries on the play and all conjecture about the secret intention behind the commentators' comments. One may, as I understand it, ask an author for information on points of detail — but that in itself is a sign of some deficiency in the work or some failure in understanding on the part of readers or audience. In actual fact, people want to know *more* about it, or something else entirely.

Everyone wants to collect confidences, or forced confessions. No-one wants to believe in spontaneous confessions, and these are the true ones.

ABOUT THE CRISIS IN THE THEATRE

Does it really exist, this crisis in the theatre? If we go on talking about it, we shall bring it into existence. It is thought that drama cannot exist in a divided society. It can exist *only* in a divided society. It can exist only when there is conflict, when I am divorced from those who govern me or those I govern (and this goes beyond the notion of social classes), my wife or my mistress, my children and myself, myself and my friend, myself and myself. There will always be division and antagonism. That is to say, there will always be division as long as there is life. The universe is in a perpetual state of crisis. Without crisis, without the threat of death, death alone remains. And so: there is a crisis in the theatre only when the theatre fails to express a crisis.

There is a crisis in the theatre when there is stagnation, when experiment is rejected, when ideas are barren, or in other words dictated. Two dictatorships threaten us. The passive dictatorship of routine; and the active dictatorship of dogma which, though apparently a moving force, is already quite automatic.

SUB-REALITY IS REALISTIC

And yet, what a wealth of space there is within us. Who dares to adventure there? We need explorers, discoverers of unknown worlds, which lie within us and are waiting to be discovered.

Sergeant-majors from right and left try to give you a bad conscience if you go out to play, but it is they who should have a bad conscience for killing the mind with boredom. Everything is political, we are told. In one sense, yes. But politics aren't everything. Professional politics destroy the normal relationship between people and alienate; commitment amputates man. It is the Sartres of this world who are responsible for alienating our minds.

It is only the feeble-minded who think that History is always right. As soon as one ideology becomes all-powerful, History has made a mistake.

The avant-garde can please neither the right nor the left because it is anti-bourgeois. Societies that have ossified, or have started ossifying, cannot accept the avant-garde. Brecht's drama is the kind of drama that finally crystallises the myths of an official religion guarded by inquisitors and in full process of petrifaction.

We should go to the theatre as we go to watch football, boxing or tennis. Indeed, a sporting match gives us the most exact idea of what the theatre is in its purest state: live antagonism, dynamic conflict, the motiveless clash of opposing wills.

Abstract thesis against abstract anti-thesis, without synthesis: either one adversary has completely destroyed the other or one force has driven out the other, or else still disunited they co-exist.

MEMORANDA

Monday

My contemporaries irritate me. I detest the neighbour to my right, I detest the neighbour to my left. Above all, I detest the one on the floor above me. Just as much, anyway, as the one on the ground floor. (Good Heavens! I live on the ground floor myself!) Everyone is wrong. I envy people whose contemporaries were alive two centuries ago . . . No: they are still too close to us. I can be indulgent only to those who lived well before Jesus Christ.

And yet when my contemporaries die, I feel terribly distressed. Distressed? Scared rather, tremendously frightened. That is understandable. I feel more and more alone. How can I manage without them? What am I going to do, living on with all 'the others'? Why is it 'the others' did not die instead of them? I wish I could make the decision myself and choose those who should remain.

Tuesday

On the telephone: 'Oh darling, are you really in Paris? . . . What a surprise, what a marvellous surprise! . . . We're so pleased to be in touch with you again . . . it's such a long time

. . . how the years go by . . . it's so long ago . . . Why yes, my husband's here . . . And the child's grown up. And yours? . . . You're not far away? . . . We'll expect you. Do come . . . come at once . . . Put them off . . . We'll put our people off too . . . There's nothing important to-day except you . . . How we've missed you in the last few years. We couldn't tell you everything by letter . . . oh, we're really so happy, you know, terribly happy . . . we've got such a lot to tell one another! So many things! . . . '

She arrives, with 'him'. Effusions. After a minute or two, we are bored, bored to death! . . . And we've missed all our engagements for the day . . . and they were *so* interesting,

It would be nice if one could read this news item in the paper: 'The plane in which Mr. X and his family were travelling has crashed. The aforesaid persons rose above the ruins of the machine and went straight up to Heaven. While permanent accommodation is being sought for them, all mail can be sent, addressed with their names, poste restante, box number . . .

Mr. X's children, who are preparing their school-leaving examinations, will continue their studies by correspondence-course.'

Wednesday

History seems to me to be a continuous series of aberrations. It is always conflicting with 'truths'. As soon as an idea, a conscious intention, tries to find realisation in history, it becomes something monstrous, the very incarnation of its opposite. The contradictions in history and society could be merely a reflection of those which grow up between conscious thought and all the obscure tendencies that go to oppose the realisation of this thought or idea. Is this man making fun of himself? Or is it a god making fun of man? Is it that all consciousness is automatically hypocritical? Is it that man always declares he wants to do the opposite of what he really, profoundly and obscurely desires to do, 'ideology' being nothing but an alibi that springs from his insincerity? But if we declare we really want to do something, if we express some thought or intention, this must surely also mean that there is some part of ourselves which really has this intention, that we are *sincerely* inspired by this idea of ours, that we *do* believe in it notwithstanding. And yet we think we believe only a part of what we really believe and want only a part of what we really want: our *dark desires*, those we have no control over, seem to be the most powerful, the most imperious. It is they which falsify and contradict our clearly expressed intentions, it is they which finally win the day, it is they which make history. How can we become conscious of our contradictions, and make them at least equal in strength? We should have to carry out historically, at the very same moment, a sort of double idea, an intention and its opposite; we should have to understand that when we desire something, it is also (and perhaps above all) its opposite that we desire; and realise the whole process in all its vibrant internal contradiction.

There are a few individuals whose conscience stands guard over a kind of truth. What kind? Difficult to define. In any case, something that is consistently opposed to History. So that the truth could be whatever goes against History. Its truth or its anti-truth. The conscience of these rare individuals attempts to straighten out the aberrations of History, which the vast majority actually consider to *be* justice and truth. Most people like to admit established facts; yet by appealing to History, they are really flying in the face of History and abolishing History. As historical truth is aberration, it would appear that all truth should transcend History. If we confined ourselves to History, we should no longer have any landmarks, we should be adrift, at the mercy of 'historical' waves, swept along aimlessly by winds and tides: or else icebound in frozen History. I believe, however, there is a Pole-Star which can help us find our sense of direction. It shines far above the waves.

Thursday

Curiously enough, it is the enemies of History who finally make it. Historicists merely justify it. They justify all its fallacies. Where else would they find an image of the truth, if they did not think they could find the truth in themselves? By looking around, outside themselves? But there is nothing but fallacy outside oneself. Do we not feel that this is not the answer, that we are wide of the mark? . . .

Friday

Right. So we want the opposite of what we want. There is the wish and the anti-wish; a wish for something and an anti-wish for something. This anti-wish is revealed (for we are not conscious of it, it is hidden) by the immediate contradiction it introduces into the way ideas are actually carried out.

Thus: the French Revolution declared its intention of establishing (amongst other things) equality. It firmly established social inequality.

The Tsar was entitled the 'Little Father' of his people; in fact he was their executioner.

Christianity wanted to establish peace and charity. It stirred up wrath and fury and perpetual war. It gave fresh cause for hatred.

Revolutionaries think they want to abolish the social classes: they establish a new and tougher hierarchy.

Saturday

(Continuation of contradictions)

The Jewish people are the people 'who do not bear the sword'; here is a people of non-violence and peace. So the Jews have been accused of fomenting wars. They do not wish for conquest: so they have been accused of wanting to dominate the world. While the Nazis and their fellow travellers, who accused them of seeking universal domination, practised imperialism themselves, on their own account.

Hitler declared he wanted to lead the German people to victory and total conquest of the world, to the highest glory: he led them, as we know, to defeat, shame and death. What is remarkable is the precision and sureness of touch with which he led them there: with the hand of a master! Not one false gesture, not one mistake, not one lost second of time: what extraordinary skill! No-one could do better. Germany's most desperate enemy could never have made such a success of it. Hitler wanted what he did not want: his will lay in his counter-will; his wish was his anti-wish.

It is also true that he wanted to exterminate whole peoples and races of mankind. In this, alas, he nearly succeeded. He had, however, never expressed any wish to save them.

About progress: We say that 'things' are not going very well. We admit that 'things' are all wrong. And yet (we always say), things are a bit better than before and they will be better still tomorrow. In reality it is perfectly clear that 'things' are going from bad to worse; that the human condition is becoming more and more difficult to bear; that the dangers threatening us, above all just recently, are becoming more and more serious and that never before has life been so universally threatened as it is to-day; it is clear that science, which was to bring us security and happiness, has brought us insecurity and fresh anxieties that no man could ever have imagined. At the time of the Patriarchs things were 'almost' going well. In any case, not so badly. A lot better than to-day, that's certain. For to-day 'things' could hardly be going worse: we have only to look about us. Let us not be taken in by our own dreams and our own desires for self-deception, let us take a good look, regardless of accepted doctrines and ideas: 'things' are getting *worse and worse* . . . And the worse 'things' get the more we shall say that 'things' are getting better. I know! — 'Still, things *are* a little better', 'things are always getting *a little* better . . . ': and the better they get, the more surely we arrive at the worst. If we say that 'things' really *are* getting better after all, there is no doubt this can only be because things can't help getting worse and worse.

We can say that X . . . is having a rest. This also means that X . . . is asleep.

Then we can say: the cemetery where he is resting.

I fail to understand why we cannot say 'having a rest'. Why? Why? Yes, why? Why?

Two types of people: a) those who say that might is always right: most people are of this type. (To say that might is right is to say that history is right; to say that might is right is also to say that the person or thing we soon expect to possess the most might is always right); b) those who say that might is always wrong (that *History* is wrong). This type is far more rare, there is no point in stressing that.

Sunday

I think about Boris Vian; about Gérard Philipe. I think about Jean Wall. I think about Camus: I scarcely knew Camus. I spoke to him once or twice. And yet his death leaves an enormous gap inside me. We *needed* this just man so much. He was quite naturally on the side of truth. He was never swept away by the current; he was no weathercock; he succeeded in being a kind of landmark.

Ten or twelve years ago the death of Emmanuel Mounier had left the same gap inside me. What lucidity Mounier had! (More of a philosopher than Camus). Whatever the subject he knew how to distinguish true from false and good from bad, and he never got carried away either: he was a man who knew how to give each fact its precise place and value. He disentangled, differentiated and integrated everything.

Then I think about Atlan, who has just died. One of the greatest contemporary painters. All the time it was: 'We must meet, see you soon and I mean it'. We shall never meet again. I shall just catch a fleeting glimpse of him in his pictures: he *will* be *there*.

I am afraid of death. I am afraid to die doubtless because, without realising it, I wish to die. So what I am afraid of is this wish of mine to die.

(*Arts*, 1960)

MORE PAGES FROM MY DIARY

The word 'revolution' is badly chosen by the 'revolution-aries'. Unconsciously it helps us to see through revolutionary action, which is itself synonymous with 'reaction', for ety-mologically 'revolution' means a 'return', and is opposed to 'evolution'. For me, revolution is the restoration of an arche-typal social or political structure: it is authoritarian, even tyrannical and hierarchical; a re-establishment in an apparently different form of the forces of government; the rehabilitation of a ruling power and disciplinary spirit that had weakened because the worn-out slogans of the preceding elite was no longer able to maintain them.

'A Jew is not a man like me,' said the Nazi. 'So I have every right to kill him'. 'A Negro is an inferior being; what is more, he is a threat to me, so I must kill him!' said the white racialist—for, when one wants to kill someone, one has to put oneself in a position of legitimate defence. For the Negroes in certain African districts a white Bible-pedlar is the in-carnation of evil, of the non-human, of the diabolical. He is marked for murder. 'A bourgeois is not really a man; or at least he is a bad or dangerous man: he must be struck down', say the petty *petit-bourgeois* Marxist thinkers. Is not a bour-geois, according to Marxism, someone who has in some way lost his humanity? M. Brecht took this literally: in one of his plays the tyrants are gigantic puppets whose heads are cut off quite serenely, for no blood flows from the cardboard throats of puppets: let us kill the bourgeois, never fear, they feel nothing. The same author has tried to show us in another play that it is against nature for a man of a lower social order to experience friendship for another belonging to a class above him; if he feels such friendship it will kill him, and it will serve him right. Christians have thought they were meant to kill pagans and heretics: because, being possessed by the devil, they were dehumanised. And are not Christians in their turn *dogs* to enraged Moslems? And so on. One has the impression that throughout time religions, ideologies and systems of thought of every kind have had as their single aim the wish to give men the best possible cause for mutual contempt and massacre.

To-day, of course, we have at last succeeded in 'demystifying' racial theories and we realise that noble ideals about war were simply founded on economics. What on earth would we do if we did not still have a bourgeois to kill; and a *petit-bourgeois* to ridicule? And the *petit-bourgeois* is not a . . . 'myth', he is not just an Aunt Sally; he cannot be demystified, because he has already been . . . 'unmasked'. How could a more extraordinary scapegoat have been invented? He is there before you, you have only to stretch out your hand, you have only to take your pick. In older times, alas, Jews and Negroes didn't turn up all over the place. You had to look for your Jew or your Negro. To-day anyone can be accused of being a bourgeois or a *petit-bourgeois*, if his ideas are not exactly what you wish them to be, or if he happens to displease you: *petit-bourgeois*, a-social, reactionary, bourgeois mentality, these are the new insults, the new ways of pillorying your fellow. And those who point the finger of scorn are, of course, most often themselves *petits-bourgeois* run wild. X and Z, for example, who are typically *petit-bourgeois*, tinged by Marxist literature—for I too believe in the '*petit-bourgeois*' . . . and hate him . . .

It is not what people think that interests me, but discovering why they think what they think, what private and psychological reasons can have led them to adopt this or that idea. Only subjective conditioning is really revealing—and objectively true. Their feelings are true, but I suspect their ideas. Behind every clear thought, behind every sign of reasonable behaviour lies some secret emotion.

Demystification is in fashion. Why should we not de-mystify what remains to be demystified?

'Intellectuals'—in reality all those *semi-intellectuals* who are active in that ill-defined area half-way between philosophy and journalism—are the real plague of intellectual life: not one of them can rival the meanest pedagogue, not to speak of the obscurest laboratory assistant. And yet there they are, bustling about, strutting up and down, drivelling and scrib-bling on from café to café, from one newspaper office to the next, restless-minded *petits-bourgeois*, born followers dying to be followed; as their own skulls are crammed they are cram-mers of skulls themselves, anti-conformist conformists, be-fuddled thinkers who believe themselves clear-headed. They are as busy as flies; towed along by others, they want to do the towing themselves; weak and tyrannical, they judge without insight, pass censure and excommunicate; they try to impose ideas that are unsound because they are wearing thin, without even noticing how 'loaded' they are—and their desire to dominate 'through the mind' and 'intellectually', under cover of the best of possible motives, is strengthened by the fact that they are themselves dominated and at the mercy of a few great tyrants, who, quite untroubled by their advice, the established laws of history or their shattered analysis of the situation, have only to raise an imperious little finger for

the course of events and the face of history to be utterly transformed: what, after all, is the function of little intellectuals
if not to discover new ways of justifying events?

For among the obsessions of these semi-intellectuals there
is *History:* 'to move with the current of History'. History,
which was until quite recently the knowledge of events in
the past, has become the science of the present and the future,
a technique for prophecy, a written and unwritten Bible, a
Law, a Divinity, a Myth: and a myth that is all the more
powerful as the demystifiers themselves not only tolerate it
but wish to inflict it on us.

History is a myth for these little intellectuals just because
they are powerless; they long for power, but it is not they
who make history: it is not even they who invent the interpretations that justify events. The Great Chiefs employ two
or three anonymous secretaries who secretly secrete one or
two slogans that are then launched on the world from behind
the closed doors of propaganda bureaux at the service of govern-
ments or other administrative bodies. The little intellectuals
take note of them, imagine they have thought them up themselves, develop them and turn them into articles, lectures,
courses of instruction, books and dogma. And so the justifications go out all over the world, and their origin is forgotten.
The busy buzzing flies are of some use after all.

And History is made regardless of the rules: Chief of State
X meets Chief of State Z who meets Chief of State W who
sees Chief of State Y, and so on. They decide on the general
orientation of 'History' among themselves. We are entirely
dependent upon them. We are at their mercy. Most of them
are sergeant-majors, semi-ignorant and more or less boorish
and tough (unless they are too subtle—which weakens them

and makes them bad leaders) and, unlike the little intellectuals, they do not have a History complex, because they have real power and it is they who create events.

Some of these little intellectuals obsessed by the *libido dominandi* also concern themselves with the theatre. They advocate *didactic* drama, of course, an excellent way of acting upon others and exercising influence. But these Stalinists or Calvinists do not themselves write plays: they simply form a narrow circle of churlish young pedants—with their societies, their debates, their reviews, and their openings into a few other publications. They are not particularly fond of one thing or the other; but, of course, chiefly they detest the '*petit-bourgeois*'.

They have defended two or three authors, in order to win them over, and win them over they have. Who are the '*petits-bourgeois*'? You and me and all those who, like me, have refused to be put upon and play their little game in spite of pressing propositions, and who are also the literary rivals of these two or three accepted masters. Passed off as 'noble ideology' (which they have assimilated but to which they have contributed nothing), basically it is petty rivalry in the world of letters that inspires these authors to repudiate the rest in the name of their religion, to which they have moreover only just been converted; and behind the pedants there is this will to power of which we have already spoken. These same pedants had, at the start, passionately flown to my defence too: then, as I did not wish to surrender completely and follow them all the way in their educative ambitions, they suddenly turned into my sworn enemies. It is also true that I attack them. And then they imagine that if I repudiate *them*, the little intellectuals, it is *the intellectuals* I am challenging, for naturally there can be no other incarnation of intellectuality except themselves, and they publicly brand me as a 'Poujadiste', after the name, I believe, of another pedant whose doctrines are very different from theirs.

Oh! If once in their lives these people ever held positions of authority, what havoc would there be, what abuse of power, what autodafés! The theatre of education would blossom out officially . . . and whoever says education also means 're-education' for those who refuse to be educated . . . surveillance . . . and prison . . .

It can't be helped, whatever may happen, I can never be so presumptuous as to claim to *educate* my contemporaries. I do not teach, I am a witness; I do not explain, I try to explain myself.

I do not write plays in order to tell a story. Drama cannot be epic . . . since it is dramatic. For me a play can never just show how a story unfolds: this would be novel-writing or film-making.

A play is a construction made up of a series of states of consciousness, or situations, which grow more intense, more concentrated, and then knit together either to be unravelled or to end in inextricable and unendurable confusion.

And why all this debate?

Obviously, the longer I live, the more tied I feel to life. I sink ever deeper into it, I am caught up in it, bogged down in it, trapped by it. I go on eating, eating, eating: I feel heavy, torpid, comatose. Once I was like a knife-blade slicing through the world, flying through existence. No longer as in the past does the universe still seem astonishing, strange and unexpected. It seems to me quite 'natural'. How hard it will be for me to tear myself away! I have grown used to it; grown used to living. I am less and less prepared to die. How painful it will be for me to loosen all the bonds that have grown up over a lifetime. And no doubt I shall not be here much longer. The greater part of the journey has been completed. One by one, it is time for me to start untying all these knots.

Existence has become an ever-present obsessive dream; it 'seems true'; it looks realistic. We often dream deeply, get trapped in our dreams . . . and we are woken from them abruptly, we are wrenched out of them.

A dream of universal existence, a dream of 'myself' and of 'myself and the others', which I shall no longer be able to recall. 'What did I dream about?', 'Who was I?', I often ask myself when I wake with a confused memory of something affecting, exciting and *important*, already receding beyond my grasp and sinking into dark oblivion for ever—leaving me only the regret that I can no longer remember.

If suddenly the 'reality' of this dream is taken from me— I shall die: I shall no longer remember the theatre, the world, the women I have loved, my mother, my wife or my child. This 'I' will have forgotten itself. And 'I' will no longer be 'I'.

And yet all this will have existed. Nothing can stop existence from having existed, from being inscribed somewhere, or from being the assimilated material of all future transformations.

HAVE I WRITTEN ANTI-THEATRE?

I believe that in the history of art and of thought there has always been at every living moment of culture a 'will to renewal'. This is not the prerogative of the last decade only. All history is nothing but a succession of 'crises'—of rupture, repudiation and resistance, and also of attempts to return to positions that have been abandoned (but viewed from a different angle, otherwise such a return would be 'reactionary' or 'conservative'). When there is no 'crisis', there is stagnation, petrifaction and death. All thought, all art is aggressive.

Romanticism too was an aggressive will to renewal: the simple desire to startle the bourgeois, or the battle of *Hernani*, the Romantic manifestos explaining how a truth opposed to the universal truth of classicism should be conceived and expressed, and above all the works of art themselves, in which this new system of expression was forged (this 'new idiom,' as we should say nowadays), here is clear evidence of the will to renewal, and a very genuine renewal it was.

Parnassianism rejected Romanticism in an effort to return to a new Classicism: Symbolism was opposed to Parnassianism; Naturalism to Symbolism and so on. Even at secondary school level, the History of Literature makes all this very plain to us.

The history of art.

Every movement, every fresh generation introduces a new style or tries to do so, because the artists are clearly or dimly aware that a particular way of saying things is worn out and that a new way must be sought; or that the old exhausted idiom, the old forms must be exploded, because they have grown incapable of containing the new things that have to be said.

So what we first notice about new works of art is that they are quite distinct from those that came before (providing, of course, that the artists have been adventurous and not just dull and imitative). Later these differences become less marked, and then it is above all their resemblance with much older works and a certain common identity that may be most noticeable; everyone feels more at home with them and in the end they are integrated into . . . the History of Art and Literature.

I know that in the long run it is possible to maintain that nothing new has happened at all. That there is no new current of ideas flowing through what we have been doing. I believe it is still too soon to assess whether something new has happened or not. But it may be that certain aspects of our work bear some relation to the various existentialisms; or perhaps we are continuing, each adding his little contribution, that great artistic and literary revolution of thought which, starting round the years 1915 to 1920 and still incomplete, has found expression in the latest scientific discoveries, psychology in depth, abstract art, surrealism etc.—no-one knows, no-one can know as yet whether we are the artisans of a real transformation in modes of thought or not—we still have too little perspective to judge.

An architecture of clichés.

And yet again—in the new there is always the old, and I even believe that this ineradicable element of 'oldness' may be something basic to the human spirit, an inexhaustible fund of knowledge that gives stability and strength, a guarantee

J

that we are not outside the main stream but continue to express some fundamental reality, which may change, as it is human, in its surface contours and yet not change in its essence. Romantic works of art are not in the long run so 'essentially' different from classical works: what is fundamentally human shows through different systems of expression, different 'idioms' . . . and the differences are really very slight from one decade to the next, from one half-century to another. Historical metamorphosis develops slowly; real transformations take far more time than this, before they become apparent.

If, however, something still seems to emerge fairly clearly in what we have been trying to do, it is that certain works denounce the inanity, the fatuity and the unreality of ideologies; perhaps we have recorded the death of ideologies, Right, Left and Centre. I do not approve of expressions like 'crisis or critique of language', or ' . . . of the language of the bourgeois'. This is to approach things in the wrong way, as though from the outside. It is, for example, far more likely that we are recording a kind of crisis in thought, which naturally reveals itself in a crisis of language—in words that no longer mean anything, in whole systems of thought that are reduced to monolithic dogma, an architecture of clichés whose elements are not only words like 'nation, national independence, democracy and the class struggle' but also 'God, socialism, matter, mind, personality, life, death etc.'

As systems of thought, *of every persuasion*, are nothing more than alibis, which hide reality (another cliché) from us and irrationally harness our emotions—it is obvious that our characters must be mad, unhappy, lost, stupid and conventional, their way of speaking absurd, their language as disintegrated as their thought. It seems to me that at this moment we are trying out a revised version of the adventure of the Tower of Babel.

'Artistic'.

And this perhaps is the message, an anti-message message, that has been brought by Beckett, a reliable witness of our times, in *En attendant Godot*, as well as by Jean Tardieu in his ironically tragic and unjustly neglected little plays, by Roger Vitrac in his early pieces, by Weingarten's explosive *Akara* and by Adamov principally in *La Parodie, Tous contre tous*, and *La grande et la petite manoeuvre;* these three plays are truthfully objective, extremely sound and lucid. Adamov has rejected these three plays, of course, because he wants a faith to believe in. But the future will judge better than Adamov whether he has been right or wrong to reject them.

And if systems of thought *of every kind* (and not just those that belong to this or that social community) lie all in ruins, what is there in these new plays that is fundamental and permanent? Derision, anguish and confusion in their purest form, and fear—in other words, essentially tragic human reality, which every now and then some doctrine or faith succeeds in masking.

It is for this reason that one can (and should) be both new and old at the same time. Perhaps our drama bears witness to this crisis (experienced psychically rather than theoretically, for after all we are 'artistic'), this *universal* crisis in thought and conviction.

The strange and the unusual.

I may add that of course, when I started writing, *of course* I wanted to 'do something new'; but that was not my method of approach. There were some things above all I wanted to say and I looked for a way of saying them that would go beyond or through or against the usual formulae. It was felt that I was being 'avant-garde', that I was writing 'anti-theatre'—vague terms, but in themselves proof that I had done something new.

A renewal of technique? Perhaps, in the attempt to broaden theatrical modes of expression by making the set and the properties act for me and by simplifying and refining the actor's style of playing. My actors were able to discover a style at once more natural and more exaggerated, something between a realistic character and a marionette: there was something strange and unusual about the natural, something natural about the strange and the unusual.

Ten years . . . is too short a time to know whether one has really achieved something. I myself shall never know. So I may die with the illusion that I have done something.

But I can affirm that neither the public nor the critics have influenced me.

From 'Reply to an enquiry',
published in *L'Express*, 1st June 1961.

IN DEFENCE OF ROLAND DUBILLARD, WEINGARTEN AND SOME OTHERS

I am often astonished at the violent indignation of certain dramatic or literary critics. It amuses me too to watch them hitting out at thin air, for as their attack is often misdirected it naturally misses the target. Nor can I really understand why they do not get indignant when, for example, the advocates of peace become, at any time it suits them, the advocates of war; when they see sensitive people who have protested against the atom bomb hold their tongues in fear or admiration if, in the name of peace, an atom bomb is exploded more powerful than all the other bombs they have so philanthropically condemned; there is no indignation either when they are told of the persecution of the friends of a man who wrote that we should respect even those who do not think as we do; if we only get indignant when *one* man is tortured, we condone terrorism and allow whole cities to be walled up and countries crushed out of existence in the name of happiness and liberty; an outbreak of collective hysteria is sanctioned in the name of reason and the 'intelligentsia', floundering in a maze of contradictions and incoherence, are stupid with rage and hatred. Death snatches at human beings at every cross-roads; nostalgia, grief, fear and our incapacity for love, not to speak of boredom, are gnawing at our hearts; the partisans of freedom turn into jailors; under the mask of virtue, the sanctimonious try to appease their envies and their jealousies, whatever catastrophes result; there is some pretence at pity for the murdered and the victims in one's own cause, but the victims of a different cause are spat upon; we all cheat, we all cheat; we mistake truth for falsehood; we can no longer recognise the truth; human relationships are degraded; the world is in a state of delirium, nothing now can hold it back in its mad tobogganing; the planet is ready to blow up and the critics—in no way indignant at all this—are indignant when they see the indignation of the poets and realise that this frenzy is reflected in their works and exposed in terms that are the very image of frenzy and delirium.

Several plays have already taken the absurd, despair and desolation as their subject. I say: they have taken them *as*

their subject. Other more recent plays, like Romain Weingarten's *Les Nourrices*, which is being played at the moment,
no longer treat desolation as a subject: they are an exact expression of desolation itself; Weingarten's play is desolation
and fear incarnate, horrifying and harrowing, a living experience of it, yet sharpened by the lucid and ironical vision
of a poet who, because he is lashing out, draws a more violent
picture of the disaster, which, being at once sinister and ridiculous, becomes all the more comic, grotesque and grandiose.
What used to be called the unity of action is destroyed in
favour of a different kind of construction: dramatic intensi-
fication springs (and this too is something new that Weingarten is contributing) from the linking-up of obsessional
images, from the language of gesture, from the freedom of
his stage "business", all these taking pride of place over the
word, which merely lends support to the dynamic imagery.
It seems to me that in the theatre of Amos Kenan, Weingarten
and Roland Dubillard dramatic expression is evolving in a
very interesting way, tending to suppress literature and thus
greatly increase its purely theatrical impact. The same process
has taken place in painting and poetry. Lamartine took grief
and melancholy *as his subject.* He wrote rhetorically. Later,
with the great symbolists, the neo-symbolists and the modern
poets, poetry became the very incarnation of grief, melancholy or delirium. Discursive language had broken down
completely and been transformed into images, direct expression, a reflecting even if shattered mirror. It is an expression
of similar purity—stripped of all that is strictly foreign to it:
literature, philosophy and speech-making—that the theatre
seems to be attaining nowadays in the work of authors ranging
from Boris Vian to Weingarten or Dubillard.

To be sure, you are not always popular if you are 'sick,' or in other words write plays that are not 'amusing' or 'positive': poets are reproached for being 'neurotic', for it is not commonly realised that it is in their 'neurosis' that the truth resides. Certainly this neurosis is not without cause. Attention should also be drawn to the serene composure of imbeciles, who remain blind, deaf and imperturbable during the worst catastrophes.

Every time it is the same old story: it is the poets who rouse the sleeping when the house is on fire and the dullards who abuse them as they wake reluctantly from sleep.

But poets *think*, imagine that! And the language in which they think is indeed the language of poetry which, transcending the thought-systems of philosophers, is an experimental and audacious idiom of research and discovery that catches a living truth. Among all those artists who are doctrinaire and dead there are a few who are opposed to doctrines and to death as well as to those who no longer wish to advance, either because they are slothfully indifferent or criminally obsessed; for life embraces more than the narrow intelligence of the ideologists, reality is more complex than their simple programmes and the solutions are outnumbered by the problems.

If Weingarten's play is, as we have seen, an exact and justifiable expression of terror, Roland Dubillard's admirable play (*Naïves Hirondelles*, at the '*Théâtre de Poche*'), is an expression of the distress we feel when confronted with a life in which we are incapable of love, with a life without purpose or lived for the wrong reasons. What are we to do about a life like this, which ages us and fills us with a boredom from which there is no escape? This is another play of anger, an anger that breaks against the walls of the impossible. This anger is in no way the same as the causeless anger in *Look Back in Anger* and a lot of other contemporary English humbug, which deplorable young English critics defend for reasons of patriotism, politics or intellectual mediocrity.

I wish I could convey the beauty of this play as precisely and powerfully as Dubillard conveys the horror of boredom. For we are not bored by this play about boredom, not do we snigger; we cry, perhaps, although there is nothing sentimental about it. Never for a moment does Dubillard mark time, the audience's interest never weakens. I am trying to fathom the author's skill in exposing the horror of boredom and analyse the way he intensifies, compresses, pinpoints and explodes it.

There is a group of characters, and they all love each other a little and detest each other a lot, try to split up and yet cannot do without each other; they hate each other when they are together, yet they sorely miss the man and woman who in the end escape, perhaps towards a new wilderness of boredom. And those who escape seem to those who remain to have been the only ones who could save them.

But this way they have of clinging to one another and yet trying to break away, of hating the person with them and longing desperately for those who have left, gives a sharp edge to their distressing need for love, which enlightens the audience about the impoverished nature of our lives.

Yes, we have acquired the habit of laughing at what should make us cry, and we do laugh at it, at least at the start. I must say too that it is because nothing happens that everything happens, that so many things happen and that this picture of tragedy and derision is complete.

There are many visual 'gags' that are comic in a sombre

way. The dialogue, which is at first unrelated to the characters and irrelevant, as if they were trying to run away from their own disenchantment (though there are revealing 'slips' and 'missed opportunities' through which we glimpse the dramatic conflict), suddenly comes to the point, the characters speak and expose themselves and the whole knot is tightened.

Some have written that the plays of Dubillard and Weingarten are rather like my own. I am very flattered. I must, however, make it clear that they do not spring from my own work. I read a play of Weingarten's in 1953. I was lucky, for if I had read it sooner I might have wondered if my own writings had not been influenced by his. Also in 1953, I saw Roland Dubillard acting in one of his 'sketches' at the '*Théâtre du Quartier Latin*': I realised he was a close relation.

Some have also said that Boris Vian's *Les Bâtisseurs d'Empire* was inspired by my own *Comment s'en débarrasser*. Actually, no-one is inspired by anyone, except by his own self and his own anguish.

But what is most striking is that, if there are several of us who see things in a similar way, if some of us confirm what the others are doing, if a new style is taking shape, there must be some truth, some objective validity in what we are writing.

Some may be delighted, others not; but you cannot stop a movement that is in evolution, the *free* and *spontaneous* expression—infinitely superior to the directives given by pedants and lay priests—of a truth that belongs to our own time, of a living art.

It is in this way that schools are born, without leaders or schoolmasters.

(*Combat*, December 1961)

J*

BY WAY OF POSTSCRIPT

We may, I think, find in The City's Coat of Arms *one of the essential keys to Kafka's thought. Here we have an interpretation, as brief as it is penetrating, of the legend of the Tower of Babel.Why, according to his interpretation, must the tower be destroyed? Why does it bring down the wrath of Heaven? Not, as one might believe, because men have tried to build the tower, but on the contrary because they really stop trying to build it: the men lose interest in the project, although they had themselves suggested it. They stop short, and get so busy organising a temporary break that they want to make it last as long as possible. They think far too much 'about signposts, interpreters and workmen's huts'. Conflicts spring up: 'each trade wanted to have the most beautiful district' and the result is 'a bloody business'. Thus secondary aims mask the principal goal and in the end pre- occupations with improving the amenities of the town completely obscure the essential problem of ultimate ends. The Goal is forgotten: no-one can now remember why he wanted to build the tower, mankind has got stuck in the mud or has gone astray in a labyrinth, the labrinth of the world.*

This theme of man astray in the labyrinth, without a guiding thread, is primordial, as we know, in Kafka's work: if man has no guiding thread, it is because he no longer really wanted one. Hence his feeling of guilt, his anguish, the absurdity of history. Anything without a goal is absurd: and this ultimate goal can only be found outside history, it ought to guide the history of mankind, in other words give it meaning. Whether we like it or not, this reveals the profoundly religious character of all Kafka's work; when man is cut off from his religious or metaphysical roots, he is lost, all his struggles become senseless, futile and oppressive.

But why in Kafka does man suffer? Because in the last resort he exists for something other than material comfort or the ephemeral: his true vocation, from which he has turned aside, must lie in his quest for the imperishable. It is the world unsanctified that is denounced by Kafka; and this is exactly what is meant by a world without Goal; in the dark labyrinth of the world, man now reaches out only unconsciously and gropingly for a lost dimension that has completely vanished from sight.

Kafka is surely in revolt against a certain identification of man with his social function, which estranges, stifles and represses a whole part (and an essential one for Kafka) of the human being. Indeed, when a general or a judge or a clerk is reduced to his function as general (or judge etc.), reduced to a uniform; when he sleeps with his uniform, only dreams of his uniform, no longer realises he is something else apart from his uniform; when a clerk is no more than a machine for filing petitions; when any one of us is prevented from existing outside our 'job' in the administration, we are dehumanised or despiritualised. But as the profound reality, the freedom, of man cannot be entirely ignored and destroyed, even when suppressed, it has its revenge: when it is not integrated into the social organisation of the City, it revolts and turns against the City, and it is this ('the closed fist' in 'the coat of arms') which will finally destroy the City. The organisation of the City connot be the true, the ultimate Goal; it may (according to Kafka, if I understand him aright), at the most be one of the means by which to attain the Goal, which is the realisation of the many-dimensioned personality of the human being: man is not Engineer, Mechanic, Local Constable, Mayor or Solicitor etc., he is simply someone who fulfils, among his other functions, the function of Mechanic etc., a function that does not contain the whole of him and cannot totally absorb him.

(Appeared in the *Cahiers Madeleine Renaud-Jean-Louis Barrault*, under the title: 'Dans les armes de la ville' . . . October 1957.)

OUTSIDE THE THEATRE

AN ANECDOTAL PORTRAIT OF BRANCUSI

I only got to know Brancusi in person in the very last years of his life, having met him in the studio of the painter Istrati. This was in the *Impasse Ronsin*, and the sculptor's studio was right opposite, just across the alley no more than a yard wide.

'Who is this Ionesco who writes plays?' Brancusi had asked Istrati. 'Bring him along one evening, I'd like to meet him.'

Of course I had admired the master's works for a very long time. I had also heard about the man. I knew he was cantankerous, not easy to get on with, grumpy, almost ferocious. With a stream of abuse he used to drive away the dealers or collectors who came to see him in the hope of buying his sculptures. With a wave of his bludgeon he also used to keep the sincere and naïve admirers who importuned him at a safe distance. And yet there were a few rarely privileged men and women whom Brancusi, unable to live always in absolute solitude, welcomed and cherished: these fortunates were invited to share his meals, which were both rough and ready and refined, consisting for example of an extraordinary yoghourt that Brancusi prepared himself, raw and bitter cabbage, salted cucumbers, polenta and champagne. Sometimes, after the dessert, when he was in a very good humour, Brancusi would give a demonstration of a belly dance in front of his lady guests sipping Turkish coffee.

I am myself bad-tempered. And that is doubtless why I detest bad temper in others. For a long time I put off going to see Brancusi: it was enough for me to contemplate his works,

266

the more so as I knew about his fundamental theories, very often explained to those who would listen to him and very often repeated by them. I had heard about his hatred and scorn for 'beefsteak' sculpture, which is what one would to-day call representational sculpture, and this means almost all known sculpture from the Greeks to the present time. I knew how fond he was of this expression and also that he loved hurling it in the faces of whoever was listening to him. The picturesqueness of his personality did not particularly attract me: he never wanted to shake Max Ernst by the hand again, because he claimed the latter had the evil eye and had made him fall down and sprain his ankle by casting hate-filled eyes upon him. Picasso too was repugnant to Brancusi, for according to him 'Picasso was not engaged in painting but in black magic'.

One winter evening I had gone to visit Istrati. We were quietly sitting round the stove when the door opened. Brancusi came in: a little old man of eighty, carrying his bludgeon, dressed in white, with a tall white fur hat on his head, the white beard of a patriarch and, naturally, 'eyes sparkling with mischief', as the common expression so well puts it. He sat down on a stool and was introduced to me. He pretended not to have caught my name. He was told it again, two or three times. Then, pointing the end of his stick at me:

'What's he do in life?'

'He's a playwright!' Istrati replied, although he had explained all this before.

'He's what?' Brancusi asked again.

'He writes for the theatre . . . he writes plays!'

'Writes plays?' said Brancusi in astonishment.

Then turning triumphantly towards me and looking me straight in the face:

'I hate the theatre. I don't need the theatre. The theatre stinks!'

'I hate the theatre, it stinks for me too. I only write plays because I don't give a damn for it. There's no other reason', I told him.

He gazed at me with his cunning old peasant's eyes, surprised and incredulous. He couldn't find an offensive enough reply straight off. He returned to the attack five minutes later:

'What did you think of Hitler?' he asked me.

'I have no opinions on that subject', I replied ingenuously.

'He was a good chap!' he cried, as though he were issuing me a challenge. 'A hero, victimised and misunderstood!'

Then he launched out into an extraordinary, metaphysical and confused eulogy of 'Aryanism'.

Istrati and his wife were shattered. I did not turn a hair. I knew that, in order to irritate his companions by taking a line he believed to be opposed to their own way of thinking, he had demonstrated one after the other his hatred first of Nazism, then of democracy, of bolshevism, of anti-communism, of the scientific spirit, of modernism, of anti-modernism, and so on.

Imagining perhaps that he was dealing with some impressionable admirer, greedy for the slightest word, or realising probably that he would not succeed in exasperating me, Brancusi gave up. He sailed into a great speech against, I was expecting it, the 'beefsteaks'; he trotted out old memories, how he had come to Paris from the banks of the Danube, making a great part of the journey on foot; he talked to us too about 'ions', sources of cosmic energy that move through space and can, he claimed, be seen with the naked eye in the rays of the sun. He turned to my wife and told her off severely for not wearing her hair long enough, and then his aggressiveness subsided. Suddenly he was filled with child-like joy, his expression relaxed, he stood up, hobbled out on his stick, leaving the door open to the cold air, and came back a few minutes later holding a bottle of champagne: he had nothing against us now, he liked us.

Later I was privileged to see Brancusi again, four or five times before his death. After a stay in hospital for a fractured leg, he could no longer leave his studio. He had a vacuum cleaner, the latest model. But when he had a lady visitor, he jumped at the chance of asking her to sweep out his studio with a real broom. He had a telephone on his bedside table, and also a little bag of tiny pebbles. When he got too bored and wanted to chat with his neighbour, he took a handful of pebbles, opened the door and threw them against his neighbour's door to call him: it never crossed his mind to telephone.

He was very near his end when my wife and daughter, who was eleven, went to see him. He was in bed, his fur cap on his head, his stick within reach. My wife is still very moved by the memory of this last visit. When Brancusi caught sight of my daughter, he was overcome with emotion. Half joking and half serious, he made her a long declaration of love. He praised her for wearing her hair long, he enthused over her beautiful eyes. And this old man with the white beard, tenderly holding her by the hand, said to her: 'I've been waiting for you ever since I can remember, my little promised bride, my fiancée, and I'm so happy you came. You see, now I am very close to the Good Lord. I have only to stretch out my arms to take hold of him.'

Then he had a bottle of champagne opened to celebrate his betrothal.

One might suppose Brancusi to have been a rudimentary

artist, instinctive and unpolished. But his work, which is both simple and subtle, is an expression of artistic (hence philosophical) thought which is infinitely lucid, highly developed and profound. His art is the expression of a highly intellectualised creative vision. Yet it is above all creation. Devoid of what is called 'culture'; standing aside from what passes for 'the intellectual life of his period', which is nothing but journalism or academic formulation, Brancusi was still in other ways incomparably more cultivated than those men of letters, those 'thinkers', those freshly-trained pedants who hang the qualification 'intellectual' round their necks and understand nothing, being far too bewitched by the simple or complex slogans they mistake for truths or for their own personal reflections. Brancusi was far more knowledgeable than Doctors of that kind. He was the liveliest expert in the problems of art. He had assimilated the whole history of sculpture, had mastered, transcended and rejected it; rejuvenated, purified and reinvented it. He had extracted its very essence.

In this century we have of course managed to rediscover the essence of painting, perhaps by methods of approximation, by gradually eliminating impurities, everything non-pictorial. This development was due to the more or less objective thinking of painters who, like critics, studied the works of others and achieved purity by a process of abstract reasoning and trial and error, although they never succeeded in grasping the essence of painting as Brancusi had grasped the essence of sculpture. In any case, for painting it was a long road lined with mistakes, where discoveries were often due to chance, to the luck of the chase, to long shots aimed at random first in one direction, then in another. And above all it was the result of the efforts of a large number of painters, two or three generations of artists, who experimented with varying degrees of accuracy.

There was no inaccuracy, no groping with Brancusi: there is perfect assurance in the development of his work. It is in himself, all alone, that he found his own models, his sculptural archetypes. With him there was an inward concentration and purification. He also looked outwards: not at pictures or statues, but at trees, children, birds in flight, sky or water.

He was able to catch the idea of movement without recourse to any particular realism and so comes closer to universal reality. His art is true: realism cannot be; at least it is surely less true. But Brancusi's school was his own thinking, his own personal experience, and not the studios of any master: he was not helped by others. He was to be very mistrustful of others.

Brancusi has been spoken of as one of the creators of non-representational sculpture. Brancusi claimed that he was not non-representational. And in fact he was not. His works are a representation of essences, a concrete image of ideas, the expression of an anti-abstract universal reality. There is nothing more concrete than his bird in flight, palpable and dynamic, the very *form* of dynamism. Rodin could express movement by giving to a certain body, to arms and legs, attitudes suggestive of motion through space. But it was still bound up with the particular. Brancusi shook off all particularity, just as he shook off all psychologicality, in order to achieve his concrete essences.

One important tendency in non-representational painting aims at expressing the poet's temperament, his individuality, his emotions, his subjectivity. We may thus distinguish one painting from another according to the particular anguish of each painter, an anguish that has become the very idiom of the painter. Brancusi's work is solely an expression of ideas and sculptural forms. We know that the poetry of Mallarmé or Valéry was a reflection about poetry. To a great extent the sculpture of Brancusi is also a reflection about sculpture; and at the same time a purely sculptural method of thinking the world, translated into living forms and lines of force.

Anti-psychological, Brancusi's art is absolutely objective: his works are testimony that cannot be refuted, sculptural testimony that goes beyond allegory.

That Brancusi willed himself not to yield to the temptation of sentimentality appeared very quickly in his work, as well as his scorn for the anecdotic or the interpretative. I know why he could not love the theatre.

In his very early works, a head of Laocoon for example, it is above all the accuracy of detail that preoccupies him rather than the expression of pain, which still comes over strongly although suggested indirectly; in his 'Nude' of a man (a study for the competition held for the final diploma at the Beaux-Arts), 'his realism' is pushed so far that it seems inhuman, owing to his total indifference to the psychology of the sculptured figure; the same thing is true of 'Flayed Man', where all that appears is his careful knowledge of the human body, presented with a kind of objective cruelty that is scarcely even ironical.

As early as 1907 (in his 'Prayer') all that is left of the emotional disappears thanks to the somewhat byzantine stylisation, which transposes and integrates the sentiment. A quick glance shows some resemblance between 'The Egg', and 'The new-born baby' in his swaddling clothes. By 1910, the '*merveilleux*' of his 'Magic Bird' has far outstripped the non-miraculous bird of realism; perhaps one can still see, by tracing the different stages of simplification, how the Egg had its starting point in the New-born baby; again one can trace the various stylisations of 'Mademoiselle Pogany' through to the final version, which is a bold and magic transfiguration. But soon, in so far as style is after all itself anecdotic, Brancusi will have gone beyond stylisation to arrive at an idiom that transcends idiom and even style. And all this has surged up from the deepest springs of his being, a continual series of extraconscious revelations, grasped with a lucidity, awareness, precision and intellectual force that make Brancusi the exact opposite of a Douanier Rousseau. Looking at 'Bird in space' in all its purity, we are amazed at the acuity of his sculptural vision, amazed at his simplicity and amazed too at our own failure to see what is so self-evident.

Very surprising, incredible, these syntheses: folklore that is unpicturesque, reality that is anti-realistic; figures that surpass the figurative; science and mystery; dynamism in petrifaction; ideas made concrete or turned into matter, visible essence; native intuition transcending culture, academics and museums.

(Appeared in '*Le Musée de Poche*')

GÉRARD SCHNEIDER AND PAINTING

You want to take up painting? It's very simple.

For painting buildings, you take a large brush and a pot of paint. You dip the large brush in the pot and you cover the ceiling and walls with paint. There is, however, one slight difficulty of course, which you should take into account. The paint must be spread out evenly, giving just one tone. It must all be a perfect monochrome. If you paint your apartment in salmon pink, it is better to have the same salmon pink round the windows and over the mantelpiece. If you have a salmon pink here and a strawberry pink there, something is wrong: unless you have done it on purpose or try to pass it off as deliberate afterwards. But no-one will want to believe you. So it is better to take lessons in painting buildings with Klein.

For representational painting, whether you are doing a portrait or a landscape, it is at once much easier. You have indeed nothing to fear from the hazards involved in the even texture of monochromy. Landscapes and portraits may and should even be polychrome, and polychromy quite naturally brings out tonal values. To make your picture, then, you gaze quite simply and attentively at the subject you are painting, and you merely have to reproduce what you see. This was the way of Velasquez, Rembrandt, Fra Angelico, Courbet and many others. It is almost childish.

If you believe you are painting only what you think you see, you have already reached a high degree of subtlety, which may even prove dangerous, for then, in the name of subjectivity and the optical and interpretative freedom this engenders, you can allow yourself to play all sorts of tricks with reality. And this is the way to come in contact with the truth. For art, believe it or not, is the truth. Photography is, they say, a minor *art:* why? Just because photography plays tricks. It would take too long to explain. For you to understand, let me just remind you that photography is above all documentary. And everyone knows that all documents are false, naturally misleading or deliberately forged.

Now if you want to make a painting of the kind indicated by the term non-representational, it is even simpler. No more worries about an even monochrome, no need either for any kind of external model.

This is how one proceeds, or rather this is how, for example, Gérard Schneider proceeds.

He starts with a spot of colour, some tone that appeals to him, a theme or foundation; this spot of colour inevitably calls up another, complementary or contrasting. A kind of dialogue takes shape. Other chromatic voices or characters intervene and play a part in this combination or composition or construction, which gradually, and still quite simply, becomes more complicated, if I may so express myself, as all the elements branch out, interweave and are unified again: the conversation continues, the murmuring of the waves or the crowds intensifies, new forces come into play and oppose one another, battles ensue, allies are sought, ruptures take place; everything has its echo, its repercussions, grows and is transformed, settles and consolidates, checks and balances, constitutes a universe of sonorities, voices, passions, forms, powers, volumes and colours; and it all goes to make up a world that is *of* this world and *out of* this world, a world kept in equilibrium by the dynamic interaction of its component parts or the clash of events, an 'edifice' that is therefore not the world but an imitation of the world; and yet a world all the same, like a world crystallised into an ideal image of the world.

I am sure that no-one who reads the last few lines will know with any certainty whether I have been trying to give an idea of the formal structure of a pictorial, musical, architectural or dramatic work of art, or even an account of tactics in a battle.

By analogy, it is almost in the same way that I myself try spontaneously to construct a play. The creative process, the archetypal composition of works of art and of imaginary worlds is in essence identical: only the materials used to construct them differ; or the languages used to express one and the same idea. As there is basically in all of us something of a painter, a musician and an architect, we have only to choose the material or the medium that suits us best and use it according to innate laws which we have only '*quite simply*' to discover in our own minds.

To proceed like Schneider is therefore still very very simple : you have only to look into yourself, never outwards; and then to exteriorise, to give expression to what is inside you, what you have seen and heard there, and allow it free play. In this way it is the world itself, as it is, that you will succeed in revealing, authentically, whereas if you only looked outside yourself, you would merely get confused, alienate both aspects of reality and make it incomprehensible to others and to yourself.

And this is how one realises that the internal is external and the external internal; that 'non-representational' is only a figure of speech, for it is simply another sort of representation, pared down but just as concrete. All pictures are representational and all pictures are non-representational, since all painters are seeking, organising and expressing the resemblances, contrasts, tonal values, intensity and degree of coldness or warmth which exist in colours. For it is clear that the landscape artist was only pretending to absorb what he saw outside: in fact he was looking at himself. In the same way the non-representational painter, while looking at himself, gazes outwards at the universe of all mankind and catches, abstracts and expresses its lines of force and active energy in all its purity.

And then of course we realise that what seemed simple is not simple at all. That it is difficult to reveal oneself to oneself; that it is far from easy to throw off what has been learnt by heart — cholesterol in the arteries of the mind — what is known and badly known when it is not an intimate rediscovery; that so-called objectivity, which is deceptive and tendentious.

So Gérard Schneider lets the keen sap rise, emerge, take shape, and enter dynamically into an integrated whole, which absorbs the pressure of this broad flood of life, so that its violence is not diminished, but balanced by counter-forces of equal power.

Gérard Schneider's genuine and essential objectivity lies hidden in his own profound subjectivity, then stands revealed and purified.

For the great artist is truthful. Art is truth. Art and science alone are truth. The rest is literature, politics, ideology, morality: particular or tendentious truths, insincerity.

Schneider's mastery consists, among other things, in allowing his spiritual energy to flow free and undefiled, to develop and, as it changes, to strengthen in growth and structure. But his surging spirit does not become rigid or static; it will not lose its way or dissipate itself in indeterminate, undirected and formless evolution. Nor does it spin round in circles, centred on itself, which is another way of cutting oneself off from the infinite progress of the mind. In what appears to us at first to be chaotic we can indeed discern certain constants, if we look with some attention at the variety of shifting shapes and colours. These shapes are colours, these colours shapes.

Thus Schneider catches movement to the life, or rather he follows movement, and we feel that his pictures extend beyond their frame, that the same variations will be played out and repeated in other realms of space, transformed perhaps, yet still having the same relationship to certain constants.

Schneider's painting therefore has an objectivity that is absolute and universal; it escapes from historicity, for it is a

monumental orchestration of history itself. Schneider's art is
both the self self-observing and the self observed.

If we say that Schneider starts with one tone of colour and
simply awaits the appearance of another, spontaneously called
up by the first, and so on, this is perfectly true. If we say that he
consciously makes an orchestral arrangement of tonal values,
knows what it will look like and knows how to produce it,
this also is quite true. For everything is calculated and nothing
is calculated. Schneider's art is exploration, and the act of
exploration brings awareness. His painting is paradoxically
both order and chaos, it moves between the two.

Being an expression of reality, his art cannot be realistic, for
realism is merely a shallow, conformist and particular expression of the real. Each one of these pictures is Schneider's own
soul and a complete new world.

If I were an art critic I could perhaps not only say that
Schneider's painting seems to me an expression of force, but
also explain *how* this force is conveyed to us plastically. Then
perhaps I could explain how it comes about that there is no
undynamic or dead space in his canvases. Perhaps I could explain how the whites accentuate the tall, black, soaring shapes,
how the yellow tints extol them and the greys tone them down
or vary their rhythmical intensity. Or how splashes of red and
yellow set a green shape in motion and how the attraction
exerted on them by long taut streaks of immobile black and
grey seems to increase its momentum. Or how it happens that
the black is strong and implacable when supported by the red,
although the white is still stronger and repels it. And again I
would say that such surging movement is possible only because it can burst out and riot through space that has depth, and
just the depth required. And how it is that sometimes, as in the

picture before me, the colours are no longer opposed, or only oppose and complement each other in a more subtle manner, creating a general air of relaxation, a feeling of release and freedom in the co-existence of forces no longer locked in battle. For the power emanating from these pictures is severe yet serene, an image of universal objective reality, pitiless yet without brutality, power that has found balanced expression in a violence that is not harsh, tragic but full of life.

Why are Gérard Schneider's pictures major works of art? This is what I have tried to indicate. Because they give us — and through a medium that is purely pictorial — an objective vision of the world, discovered through his own deeply sub-jective experience, in other words in a spirit that reflects the world or is itself in the world's image. As we tried to say at the start, the ultimate revelations of art coincide with those of philosophy and science, whose truths, differently expressed yet essentially identical, cannot but corroborate one another.

(Appeared in the review '*Le XXe siècle*',
January 1961)